Grace Notes

Jan 2024

Spirituality and the Choir

M. Anne Burnette Hook

DISCIPLESHIP RESOURCES

P.O. BOX 840 • NASHVILLE, TENNESSEE 37202-0840

www.discipleshipresources.org

Cover design by Lori Haley; book design by Sharon Anderson

ISBN 0-88177-242-9

Library of Congress Catalog Card No. 98-70471

DR242

TABLE OF CONTENTS

SECTION ONE: SPIRITUALITY 101

SECTION TWO: MORE ABOUT THE MEANS OF GRACE

SECTION THREE: GETTING STARTED

CHAPTER 1:

"I'm not religious; I'm spiritual!"

The phone rang in my office while I was sorting through handbell music. "It's my wife, Linda," Carl said in a rush from the other end of the line. Linda was a member of the choir. "She's been assaulted at gunpoint in our home. She wants to talk to someone but doesn't feel comfortable with the pastors. Can you come over?"

While the details of the conversation may be different, many leaders of choirs have experienced similar circumstances. The spouse of a choir member dies. An alto goes through a difficult divorce. The child of a handbell ringer is indicted on drug charges. A singer is experiencing depression.

Those of us who are called into church music, whether as a full-time, part-time, or volunteer vocation, often have a wide variety of musical resources on which to draw—advanced degrees in church music, years of experience singing in a choir, and plenty of continuing education opportunities available to help us with the musical aspects of our work. How many of us are sufficiently prepared for the other part of our calling, that of being a spiritual leader for the choir members?

"But I'm not called to be a spiritual leader; I'm not equipped to be one," you may be thinking. "And besides that, my singers don't come to choir to be spiritual; they come to make music." That may very well be true for many of the people who come to your rehearsals. But what is also true is that the people who come to your rehearsals are not musical robots but spiritual beings, people who are filled with needs and desires, with joy and pain. They come to make music, yes; but they also come to church seeking an experience of God, and they hope to find both through participation in the choir.

Spirituality in the Culture

Your choir members are not alone. Seeking for God is currently a popular activity. A quick surf of our culture shows that almost everyone is in on the action. Magazines such as *Time* and *Newsweek*® have featured articles on spiritual issues such as the historical Jesus and the existence of heaven. Television shows range from news reports on the phenomenon of contemporary worship, to roundtable discussions on the meaning of the stories in Genesis, to dramas featuring angels intervening graciously in the lives of unsuspecting humans. *The New York Times* Bestseller Lists for the last several years have included titles dealing with spiritual and self-help issues. The Internet contains a staggering range of possible web sites dealing with spiritual things (320,985 on Christian spirituality alone the last time I checked), including a site where you can make your confession online. You can even call your own personal psychic for $3.95 a minute. Spirituality is truly a hot topic.

Surveys indicate that many adults in the United States consider themselves highly spiritual. Most adults want a close relationship with God. However, membership and attendance in mainline churches continue to drop steadily. People are moving away from traditional, mainline Protestant denominational religious expression to an independent, nondenominational, nonexclusive, increasingly pluralistic spirituality. It is quite fashionable nowadays to say, "I'm not religious; I'm spiritual." And, in many cases, the focal point of one's beliefs is as unique as the individual purporting to believe in it.

Why are we experiencing such a renewed interest in spirituality? In every century, history has recorded that humans have sensed that the end times were here. Yet in generations before, the possibility of extinction by our own hands through nuclear annihilation has not had the same reality that it does for those of us who grew up during the Cold War. Thus, more people are focusing on these days as the *real* end times. Apocalyptic literature from everyone from fundamental Christians to New Agers predicts that the end of the world will come within our lifetime. Fringe groups gather their disciples in shelters or mountain retreats or mansions in southern California to await the event. For the rest of us, the very real threat of violence in our world leads us to long to escape from this age into a new earth free from war, violence, pollution, poverty, and all the ills that plague our existence. Whether we believe that these are the end times or not, this heightened awareness makes us more contemplative of our own spiritual nature.

Others would say that the maturation of baby boomers is contributing to the increased interest in spirituality. Baby boomers reached adulthood from the sixties (the sexual revolution) to the eighties (the me decade). As they approach middle age and looming elderhood, they realize that freedom from responsibilities and the accumulation of material goods have not brought fulfillment. They are turning to spirituality for answers to their question of life's meaning.

Some have turned (or returned) to mainline Protestant denominations in the last decade for answers to their meaning-of-life questions. Many have also left the church again after not finding what they were looking for. Although the church seems the logical place to search for such answers, unfortunately the church has not always known what to do with seekers other than to get them involved in the institution. You're looking for God? We put you on a committee. In worship, the practices of traditional church worship do not always allow for experiences of God outside the narrow order of the worship bulletin. In addition, people who do experience God in vital ways often do not find places to expand on their experiences within traditional church settings. Indeed, the goal of institutional Christianity for the last several decades seems to have focused more on church membership and church growth than discipleship and spirituality. We appear to have said, "It is okay to search for God as long as you don't find God," as the joke goes. As a result, these folks searching for God have turned away from the church for guidance and to a variety of spiritualities, ranging from gender and cultural sects to New Age groups.

Certainly another factor affecting the current face of spirituality is American rugged individualism. Citizens of the United States take great pride in the rights and freedom of the individual, and this belief spills over into the spiritual realm as well. Spirituality is largely perceived as what one makes it; adherence to any specific belief system or practice is irrelevant, just as long as one is generally a good person, does things for others occasionally, and commits none of the really big sins, such as murder and burning the American flag. This is particularly true of the baby boomers, the generation who decided early on that the only people they could truly trust were themselves. Thus, the religion and spirituality of the rugged individualist lean toward belief in a God of his or her own making.

Certainly the current interest in spirituality is complex, not to be explained away with one or more superficial reasons. Whatever the reason, it is a topic of high interest and speculation. For those of us in leadership positions within mainline denominations, this interest poses both a challenge and an opportunity. Our challenge is to accurately portray Christian spirituality—rooted in the gospel of Jesus Christ and shaped by the experience of those saints who have gone before us—as unique among other spiritual offerings, different from and more lasting than the various spiritualities of the day. Our opportunity is to be able to offer the great love and grace of God to people who are hungry and thirsty for the nourishment that the Word of God can provide. "The fields are ripe for harvesting" (John 4:35) in ways they haven't been before.

Making Disciples for Christ

In April 1996, the General Conference of The United Methodist Church made a historic pronouncement: that the purpose of the church is "to make disciples of Jesus Christ" (*The Book of Discipline of The United Methodist Church—1996*. Copyright © 1996 by The United Methodist Publishing House; page 114. Used by permission). I remember much of the reaction to this statement: "Well, duh! It took action by General Conference to say that?" In some ways, the response is justified. After all, Jesus' parting words for the disciples were for them to "go therefore and make disciples of all nations, baptizing them in the name of the Father and of the Son and of the Holy Spirit, and teaching them to obey everything that I have commanded you" (Matthew 28:19-20a). If The United Methodist Church, or any Christian church for that matter, does not have making, forming, and deploying disciples for Jesus Christ as its foundational mission, it is, sadly, far off the mark.

Yet the statement made by General Conference was also necessary to articulate. At one time in our society Sunday morning was a sacred time, left open for worship attendance. Business and non-church activities kept their distance from this time. Today in some regions of our country, malls open on Sundays at the same time they open on the other days of the week, and youth athletic teams hold weekly practice sessions on Sunday mornings. Although Sunday may still be considered a family day, church attendance is more often viewed as one of many good things to do on that day. In this cultural climate where churches are competing with so many other good and attractive things for people's time and participation, the church may be tempted to enter into the contest using the world's standards. If we consider the parable of the lost sheep, we realize at once the mistake of using the world's standards to attract people to Christ. The shepherd didn't make the sheepfold more attractive with better facilities or the right kind of music in order to draw the lost sheep home; he went out in search of the lost sheep. If we are to follow in Christ's path, we too must go out in search of "sheep" rather than relying on our reputation of friendliness, church league basketball, recreational facilities, or even excellent music programs to attract them. We attract people so that we might share the good news with those who need to hear it. The task of the church is not to build better, more attractive institutions but to make disciples of Jesus Christ.

While the statement "to make disciples of Jesus Christ" is both noble and relatively easy to accept and understand, it is also somewhat difficult to define. I suspect that every church would claim that they are making disciples for Christ in an active, thoughtful, and intentional way. But what does disciple-making look like? How does it manifest itself in the life, work, and calendar of a local church? How does it happen in the choir? *Does* it happen in the choir?

The Primary Task of the Local Church

I have been better able to comprehend disciple-making as the primary task of the church by understanding the process as described by Ezra Earl Jones in his book *Quest for Quality in the Church: A New Paradigm* (Discipleship Resources, 1993). He describes the primary task of the church in four parts:

- reaching out to people and receiving them as they are—creating settings where people who are seeking God can be found by God, such as worship and small groups;
- relating these people to God—sharing the good news of God's great love for them through Jesus Christ, and God's desire to be in deeper relationship with them;
- nurturing these people in discipleship—helping them understand what living as a follower of Christ involves; supporting them and encouraging them to support others through participation in small groups and outreach activities; helping them discern what their unique ministry is;
- sending these people out to live as disciples in the world for the transformation of the world—helping them live out their discipleship in their daily lives, through all of their interactions with other people, so that God uses them to touch other people's lives.

These four steps describe disciple-making as a process or system in which people enter into the church seeking God, find God (or rather are found by God), grow in their understanding of what it means to be a disciple, are nurtured in and by the community, and then are sent out to be disciples in their daily lives. They are transformed by the power of the living Christ from seekers into believers and then into disciples for Christ. We in the church understand that our call is to create settings where all of this can happen. We must also work with the Spirit in the process rather than being a constraint to the process.

This four-part statement of the primary task of the congregation may seem just as obvious as the mission statement made by General Conference.

Yet if you were to look closely at your own congregation, would you see that task clearly being lived out? I suspect that many United Methodist congregations have some ways of living out the primary task but just as many ways of not living it faithfully.

For example, when people visit your congregation and read the list of ministry opportunities for the week on the church calendar, what do they read? When they are invited to join the church, are they invited to join the congregation on a spiritual journey following Christ, or are they offered membership as a formality through transfer or profession of faith? Are new members offered the chance to participate in a small group for the purpose of faith formation, or are they put on a committee to get them involved? When was the last time your own faith was formed significantly in a committee meeting?

Jesus calls us not to assimilate members but to make disciples. This call is true for the whole congregation as well as for every segment of the congregation. I invite you to think back to your congregation's weekly calendar once again. What opportunities do you see that are intentional faith-forming or disciple-making experiences? Ideally you see corporate worship and Sunday school, Bible study classes, small groups for all ages, and various opportunities to serve others in the community.

Examine the calendar again. What events on the calendar have as their purpose something other than faith formation? Finance, trustee, and other committee meetings; church athletic league practices and games; choir rehearsals; and other task- or activity-oriented groups have a purpose apart from faith formation. Certainly these groups are connected to the primary task in that they often support one of the four parts of the task. For example, creating settings where people can experience God would be more difficult without the watchful eyes of trustees maintaining the safety of the church building. Careful preparation and presentation of worship music can help worshipers experience God's presence in deep and profound ways. Being a part of these groups can also be a faith-forming experience for those who participate.

Look once again at the activities on the calendar. How many of these activities are centered on Christ, and how many are centered on the institution? Or, to put it another way, which of these activities participate actively and intentionally in the making, forming, and deploying of disciples, and which of them focus on institutional maintenance?

Let's focus more narrowly on the choir. Is the purpose of the music program in your congregation to help shape the participants so that they grow in their relationship to Christ, or does the program exist primarily to serve the music needs of the worshiping congregation? Do people who come into your choirs seek a relationship with the living God, or do they want merely an adequate musical experience? Do you as director see making disciples or making musicians as the primary goal of music in the church?

Think also about your weekly rehearsal schedule. How much time during the rehearsal do you spend on the intentional spiritual growth of the people present? Do you talk about your reasons for choosing a particular anthem for a specific Scripture reading? Do you allow opportunities for people to tell about their own faith experiences and voice prayer concerns? Does your task of preparing music for worship support or overshadow your call to form these disciples? Does the faith formation of those coming to sing enter into your rehearsal planning at all?

I believe that every segment of a congregation's life and work together must intentionally participate fully in the primary task of the church in making, forming, and deploying disciples, or it should not be a part of the church's ministry. That includes the choir; perhaps it even applies especially to the choir because of music's unique ability to help people experience God's presence in powerful ways. I also believe that the choir's work begins with the intentional spiritual formation of choir members in and through the choir rehearsal.

Now, after making such a bold statement, I also understand that the task of the choir as music leaders in worship is still a very present and worthy calling. If we were to abandon our call as music leaders in worship in order to focus exclusively on our own spiritual growth, we might as well become a large covenant group and leave the music making to someone else. But, are the faithful and careful fulfillment of our call as leaders of worship and music, and the intentional care for the spiritual growth of individuals in the group mutually exclusive of each other? Can both coexist and even flourish within the same group? I believe that they not only can but must in order for us to be faithful to God's call to be disciple-makers.

Choir as Faith-Forming Experience

The purpose of this book is to help you imagine how your choir might be both a faith-forming experience for its members and a leader in the faith formation of others through worship. The transformation process begins with a spiritual leader, one who is on the journey with the choir and who is not afraid to invite others to join in the experience. The best way to encounter God in and through the choral experience is careful and intentional use of the means of grace as they have been practiced by saints throughout the centuries and articulated by John Wesley in the General Rules of The Methodist Church. A spiritual choir leader can plan and prepare a choir program that balances both faith formation and quality musical leadership in worship. Such a program will transform those who participate in it.

In this book we will explore each of these areas. We will begin by exploring spirituality and the church, with a brief overview of Christian spirituality, a general look at the means of grace and their place in United Methodist practice, and the ways to begin practicing or to continue our own spiritual disciplines. We will then focus more specifically on the individual means of grace and their potential use in the choral rehearsal and the personal spiritual lives of choir members. Finally, we will discuss the careful balance between *doing* and *being* in the choir, the balancing act of preparing our choirs for worship and forming disciples for Christ.

You are invited to join with me in the journey. You may well be an active traveler already, or this may be a new experience for you. Perhaps you are somewhere in between the two. Wherever you are in your personal spiritual development, God is calling you to look deeper, to listen more closely, and to follow what you hear more faithfully. As a leader of others, you are also being called by God to entice others into the journey, both by the example of your own walk and by your intentional leadership of the choir.

Finally, this book is intended to prompt dialogue not only between you and the text but also between you and those people whom you minister with. We are much more likely to learn and actually use a new idea if we tell someone else of our intent. I have attended many workshops on worship and music during my professional life. Each time, I have come away with the burning desire to be more creative, more spiritual, and better organized with my music ministry; and I have vowed to try some of those new, creative ideas that I learned at the event. Inevitably the press of reality has pushed aside those good intentions and often, along with them, the wonderful ideas I learned. Only when I attended the event with someone I trusted and asked to hold me accountable did I actually incorporate a significant part of what I learned into what I did on a daily basis. We learn and grow more effectively in small groups in which we are lovingly held accountable for our actions. John Wesley called this Christian conferencing, a concept we will discuss later in the book.

Because of this reality, I suggest that you read this book within the context of a covenant group rather than in isolation. If you are not in a covenant group, I recommend that you invite other choir directors in your area to read it and discuss it as a group. Perhaps an even better group to read this with is a gathering of choir members, ones who are already on a spiritual journey or who are interested in beginning such a journey. Engage the text with your own choirs in mind, and trust in the creative action of the Holy Spirit to reveal to you ways in which you might make the choir experience a faith-forming one for people who are present.

What I know for certain is that we do not journey alone. We travel with those saints who have gone before us, those saints with whom we live and work, and, most of all, the presence of the One who does not send us to a new place but rather calls us to where he already is, the Living God made known to us in Christ Jesus.

Questions for Reflection and Discussion

1. Remember a time when you were called upon by a choir member to be a spiritual leader for that person. Did you feel equipped to act in that role? Why or why not?

2. Describe signs of the growing interest in spirituality in your church and community.

3. How would you define the task of making disciples of Jesus Christ?

4. Would you describe your congregation currently as a disciple-making church or a programmatic church? In what ways does it intentionally participate in disciple formation? In what ways is it programmatic?

5. What is your honest initial reaction to the idea that the life of a choir should intentionally help choir members grow spiritually?

CHAPTER 2:

What is Spirituality, Exactly?

I remember my first experience with "spirituality." I was in elementary school. My dad was pastor of a growing suburban United Methodist congregation in east Memphis. We were good friends with several families in the church, but one family in particular seemed to consider us especially close friends for a short while. The children were close in age to me and my siblings. The kids stayed with us once for several days during the school week when their parents were out of town, a rare and unheard-of treat for us.

I don't remember exactly what happened to change our relationship. What I do remember is that sometime later, when we were enjoying our yearly Halloween ritual of trick-or-treating, this family started handing out religious tracts instead of candy. I knew that something significant had changed, and whatever it was, I also knew that I didn't particularly like it and it scared me a little.

That proved to be the beginning of a series of encounters with people in our church and community who claimed a heightened spirituality that most in our church did not seem to possess (including the pastor and his family). My mother had a conversation with one of the converts regarding a particular belief about God, to which this woman replied, "I used to believe that same way, until I had an indwelling of the Holy Spirit." Ouch!

The struggle between groups in our church and community continued rather amicably until January of 1973. During that year the Memphis City School Board revealed a plan for desegregating the school system the coming school year. The controversial plan would bus children from predominantly African-American schools and neighborhoods to predominantly white ones and vice versa. The upheaval in weeks and months that followed was often tense and confusing.

When the plan was implemented in the fall of 1973, the great "white flight" occurred. Many children in our neighborhood left the public school system to attend one of the newly formed "Christian" schools chartered after the plan was announced. When my sister boarded the bus for a midtown school, she was one of only one hundred fifty students in three grades from two neighborhoods whose families had chosen to stick with the system. Many of those who stayed in the public school system did so out of principle or because they lacked the funds to attend a private school or to move into a different school district. By the time my sister graduated, the number had dropped to what the local press called an "isolated minority."

The people we knew who chose private church schools for their children inevitably replied when questioned, "I just want the best education—a quality, Christian education—for my children; and I don't want my children to have to ride a bus." Never mind that many of these schools were unaccredited; never mind that many of the children boarded buses in order to attend these private schools. These church schools had provided them an out from having to deal with the severe inequality of life in Memphis between white people and black people, at the same time giving them a pseudo-spiritual reason for doing so. Some of these people even claimed that God provided tuition for them through some unexpected financial windfall. While I would never doubt God's ability to provide all of our needs for us, including the financial ones, I did (and still do) seriously question giving credit to God for something that seemed to me to have an evil purpose, the separation of God's people from one another because of one group's sense of superiority over another.

While the results of my family's choice to stay with "the system" on these occasions out of principle has had many graceful, lasting effects, one early result for me was clear: I realized that people I knew who claimed to be spiritual used their spirituality as a weapon for sin, either as a club with which to beat non-believers (whom they defined as all who did not believe the same way they did), or as a fence to keep them safely protected from the undesirable ones. Therefore I rejected spirituality, at least as I had observed it, as a false teaching.

Another result was that my family and I surrendered the words and phrases from our own tradition that were used so freely by these people, such as *prayer* and *the Holy Spirit*. We did not mean them in the same way and did not wish to be confused with more narrow positions. We continued to pray at meals and in private, to attend worship regularly, to be committed to acts of service and mercy in our daily lives, and to li sistently with our beliefs; but we were not, thank you very much, sp

The Rest of the Story

That attitude continued within me throughout my growing up years. I went to seminary, which pretty much reinforced my intellectual relationship with God. I got my first church music job, and then my second. I enjoyed life, dealt with problems as they came along, prayed to God because I knew that's what Christians did, and tried to live my life as I thought God would want me to. Then it happened.

"It" could have been anything: the death of a loved one, a disabling accident, a painful divorce. For me it was the breakup of my engagement ten days before my wedding. I was devastated—lost, empty, alone. For the first time in my life I realized what little comfort my beliefs about God gave me in the face of a crisis. I had a wonderful support system in friends and family, but even they could not ease the pain I felt. I never doubted the existence of God or God's love for me. I even knew (intellectually) that God was suffering with me, but that didn't seem to lessen the intense feeling of failure and loss I was experiencing.

And then grace appeared. Grace was in the form of a counselor who suggested that I use the time of pain for learning and growth. He encouraged me to read better literature, exercise regularly, and, most importantly, begin to develop a spiritual life. I joined a therapy group that focused on dream interpretation. I joined a class at church on prayer and journaling and began to practice that discipline. I learned a great deal about myself and my beliefs.

The most profound lesson I learned is that I knew a lot about what I thought about God, but I had almost no personal relationship with God. The only exceptions were occasional conversations I had with God during which I did most of the talking. At some occasions in my life, I had experienced glimpses of the potential relationship—the certainty of God's presence with me during a particular choral anthem, the answer to my prayer for a new employment situation, the graceful moment of forgiveness when I had wronged a close friend. But these were not enough to compel me into an active relationship with God. It took a crisis in my life to send me looking for the one thing I had been seeking and thought I had lost: wholeness, healing, and the certainty that I was a loved, valuable person just for who I am.

Another lesson I learned is that I had harbored a secret, arrogant notion that people who were "spiritual" were really just avoiding the hard work of learning about God. *If they really understood God, they wouldn't need spirituality*, I

'earned is that knowing *about* God is not the same as
same way that knowing about the Prince of Wales
close personal friend of his. I knew a lot about God, or
true about God, but I didn't really know God. And
ants most from me is not for me to have all my facts and
s straight about God but to be in relationship with God.

What Is Spirituality?

Later in my life I met people whom I would describe as truly spiritual. They have a deep and sustaining relationship with the living God. They thank God for all the good things that happen to them, and they face the bad things with confidence and serenity. The witness of their lives has drawn me like a flower following the warmth of the sun into a deeper longing for what they have come to know and be. They have taught me that spirituality is not a weapon to beat people over the head with, nor is it a fence for shielding us from those we consider undesirable. It does not guarantee that good things will happen to us or protect us from the bad things that do happen. It is not about using the right words or attending a certain church. It is not the exclusive property of the Christian fundamentalist or the monk in seclusion. What spirituality is most fundamentally about is *relationship*—with God and with others.

Humans are essentially spiritual beings; that is, we were created by God to be in relationship with God. In Genesis 1:26 we read, "Then God said, 'Let us make humankind in our image, according to our likeness.' " And in Genesis 2:18 we read, "Then the LORD God said, 'It is not good that the man should be alone; I will make him a helper as his partner.' " We humans, created in the image of God, are created to be in relationship, both with God and with other people.

Throughout the Bible we find examples that illustrate the understanding and misunderstanding of what those relationships should be, culminating in the person and life of Jesus, son of God. Through both his teachings and his life, Jesus personified relationship with God. He had the audacity to talk to and about God in the most intimate of terms, even at an early age. At age twelve we find him in the Temple telling his anxious parents, "Did you not know that I must be in my Father's house?" (Luke 2:49b). How wonderful and confusing it must have been to people who were accustomed to relating to God through sets of laws and mediators to be gracefully confronted by the God who is our loving parent. This relationship is further described by the apostle Paul: "When we cry, 'Abba! Father!' it is that very Spirit bearing witness with our spirit that we are children of

God, and if children, then heirs, heirs of God and joint heirs with Christ" (Romans 8:15b-17).

Our spirituality is dependent both upon God's work within us and upon our own choices and actions. God's desire is always that we be in relationship with God, but the choice is ours to make. The great paradox of the Christian faith is that the grace and love of God are always available to us, but we must both accept and respond to these gifts for them to be real in our lives. The good news is that God never leaves us alone entirely. Lovingly nudging us from our complacency, stubborn pride, or fear of intimacy, God lures us into relationship with the promise of eternal life—one with meaning, purpose, and joy.

Spirituality as Relationship

What does it mean to be in relationship with God? There is no way to adequately or completely answer such a question. However, from both history and my own experience I can at least define some parameters. Being in relationship with God means being in conversation with the One who created us. This conversation involves listening to God prompting us through our inner voices and through the voices of those whom we care deeply about and trust completely. We hear God throughout the pages of the Bible and in the teachings and experience of the many believers who have gone before us and left us a record of their own journey with God. This conversation involves talking with God about our own joys and pain, desires and fears, entrusting these to One who loves us completely and unconditionally.

Another aspect of being in relationship with God is that we must allow that relationship to influence what we do and how we live. This relationship has a purpose: to make us more like the God who created us in God's image. The word *formation* comes into the picture here. We were formed in God's image at the birth of humanity; we are being formed continually throughout our lives by decisions we make, people we choose to relate to, influences we allow to shape us. Spiritual formation is active participation in a relationship with God, allowing the grace and love of God to so shape and mold us that we are *transformed*—"new creatures," as the apostle Paul puts it—into people who are becoming more and more the image of God.

The test of a believer's true adherence to any belief system, spiritual or otherwise, is in the way the beliefs influence behavior. For example, I believe strongly that a healthy body needs proper nutrition and plenty of exercise in order to prosper. I believe that with all my heart. I trust the nutrition and fitness experts who have studied this field. Do I eat properly and exercise regularly? Sometimes, but I am by no means a health and fitness nut. Why? Because although I believe that what they tell me is true, I just as often choose a club sandwich over a more healthy vegetable plate, and a nap over a brisk walk. I believe what they say; I just don't believe it enough to make me change my lifestyle.

If we are in relationship, however, then the beliefs take on a whole new dimension. A pregnant woman who otherwise may eat an unhealthy diet may choose the more healthy fare because her young child's well-being depends on her eating habits. A smoker may ignore warnings to his own health but may choose to quit because of secondhand smoke risks to his spouse and children. When we are in relationship, that which we do affects and is affected by the one with whom we have a relationship.

The true fruit of a vital relationship with God is evident in our choosing a godly path to follow: practicing the spiritual disciplines; living lives of personal holiness; and serving those whom God favors, the poor and those on the margins of our society.

As with other relationships, developing a deep and lasting relationship with God takes time. This is true on both a daily and a long-term basis. Today our lives seem to go faster and faster. We have developed technology and machines to do much of the work we used to have to do; but instead of having more time free for things that really matter, we seem to have less and less time. We feel trapped by the many good things that we can do, and often we feel unable to attend to the things that really matter. Oh, there are lots of tools to help make us more efficient, so we can do more. Unfortunately, those tools drag us further into the black hole of doing more work faster rather than enabling us to identify the priorities in our lives.

If developing and nurturing a deep relationship with God is a priority for us, then we must be willing to make time for it. We must schedule time for God in the same way we schedule time to be with and to nurture our relationships with our spouse, children, other family members, and close friends. Relationships take time and effort. The good news is that a relationship with God will enhance all other relationships; it will enable us to cope better with all of the things that draw energy away from the things that matter most to us.

Developing such a relationship with God not only takes daily time but also requires the lengthy space of time to develop fully. I remember a story told by Dr. Hilbert Berger, United Methodist pastor and stewardship specialist. He told of himself as a young pastor in the early 1940's. He served a small rural congregation while attending seminary two hundred miles away. He was away from his parish during the week and traveled to the community during the weekend for worship. One Friday he arrived at the train station in his town to find his young wife waiting for him in her best dress. She took him home, where he found his favorite meal awaiting him, served in the dining room on their best china. He knew that something was up, but she made him wait until after dinner was over. After dessert, again his favorite, she looked lovingly into his eyes and told him she thought it was time for them to begin their family. Berger finished the story by saying, "She stood up and went directly to the bedroom; and by the time I arrived there, she presented me with a seven-pound baby boy!"

He then concluded, saying, "Of course, it didn't happen that way, but isn't that our theology? We all know that the birth of a child takes conception and then nine months of development before the birth. Why then do we expect the birth of our conversion and relationship with God to happen instantly? It takes time and nurturing for that to occur."

A final characteristic of our relationship with God is that we do not thrive in this relationship in isolation. God has given us a world of other people also striving to be faithful to God's call in their lives. Each one is on a different leg of the journey. Some have traveled far on the path; their experience helps us to be faithful in times of stress or boredom. Some are new to the journey; their enthusiasm rekindles an awareness of why we are on the path. Others are somewhere in between, alternately offering encouragement to us and needing it from us. There are some who have not yet chosen to come on the journey; they are watching your progress, waiting to determine if the trip is worth the effort. All of these people are in our churches, in our homes, and in our workplaces.

The small groups that exist within the church, including the choir, are ideal places for seekers on the journey to offer support to one another. In the choir setting, people can swap stories and offer encouragement. They can learn—both from you as a spiritual leader and from one another—how to be more faithful on the journey. This will happen with or without your planning; however, it will happen more effectively if you plan for the choir experience to encourage that kind of faith formation.

Being in relationship with God involves God's action within us and our own response to God. It includes conversation with God. It manifests itself in a life of personal holiness and service to others. Relationship with God takes time, and it flourishes when we are also in relationship with others who are on the journey.

Different Spiritual Types

To say that we were all created for relationship with God is not to say that we all relate to God in the same manner. Certainly the diversity of beliefs among Christian denominations is testimony enough to the variety of ways in which people relate to God. Probably within your own congregation you will find people who have the same understanding of God that you do, and others who have a completely different picture of what Christianity is all about.

I led a Sunday school session on hymn texts in the last church I served. I was describing some of the beautiful imagery in Jeffery Rowthorn's contemporary text "Creating God, Your Fingers Trace" (*The United Methodist Hymnal*, 109). His poetry ignites my imagination to picture and to praise an artistic, creating God at work in the universe and in me. When I asked for comments from the class, one man said, "That hymn just leaves me cold." I was really surprised by his response. When I asked him what kinds of hymns elicited a better response from him, he said, "You know, the good old hymns, like 'Amazing Grace,' or 'Rock of Ages,' or 'How Great Thou Art'—hymns that make me *feel*!" For him, the criterion of a good hymn consisted of the ability of the hymn to draw out an emotional response; for me the text needed to say something true and worthy about God.

Does the difference in our reactions mean that I am a more thoughtful Christian than he? Does it mean that he has a closer relationship with God because he expresses his faith in emotional terms? The answer is no to both; instead, he and I have different spiritual preferences, or are different spiritual types.

In her book *Discover Your Spiritual Type* (The Alban Institute, 1995), Corinne Ware explores four spiritual types: head spirituality, heart spirituality, mystic spirituality, and kingdom spirituality. These are not stereotypes with which to label people; instead they are preferences that help us understand how people relate to God most easily. These types also explain why we often disagree with others in our church in regard to worship and music.

The head spirituality is an intellectual faith. People with this spiritual preference favor thoughtful, reasonable sermons; well-crafted hymn texts; theologically sound prayers. They appreciate fine music presented well. They like particular hymns because those hymns accurately and poetically express what they believe about God, not because of the way the music makes them feel. Choir directors who have this preference will choose an anthem for Sunday because it fits the lectionary readings, even if the choir dislikes singing it. Pastors with this type will choose a hymn that the congregation does not know because it expresses a specific idea addressed in the sermon.

The heart spirituality is concerned more with emotions than with intellect. The primary religious interests of people with this spiritual type are evangelism, witnessing, and testimonies. The focus tends to be more on the personal experience of God rather than the corporate expression of praise to God. Music in worship is important to these people because of the way it helps them feel God's presence. They tend to prefer hymns that remind them of specific faith experiences. Thus, favorite hymns of many in this category might include "In the Garden," "Amazing Grace," "How Great Thou Art," and more recently "Here I Am, Lord" and "Spirit Song." Chorally, they would choose a lively spiritual or a touching ballad to evoke specific emotional responses in the hearers. People with this type of spirituality value emotional experience over doctrinal purity, and they don't feel that they have worshiped unless they experience an emotional response.

The experience I described with the man in Sunday school is a typical clash between head spirituality and heart spirituality. Another example of this difference is evident in a conversation I had with a colleague. She is a member of a large United Methodist congregation with a traditional, formal worship service. One day she asked to have lunch with me to talk about worship at her church. She said, "I love my church. The choir is magnificent. The preaching is very good. The worship service is well crafted and the ministers are effective leaders. It absolutely leaves me cold." She was describing the tension between the church's head spirituality worship experience and her own heart spirituality preference. Neither is right or wrong; they are merely preferences.

Two other spiritual types also exist but in fewer numbers in local churches than the first two described. One of them, the third spiritual type, is mystic spirituality. The mystic prefers to experience God, as does the heart spirituality; but this experience is of the mystery of God rather than what we can know about God through our experience. Mystics focus on hearing from God rather than talking to God. Silence is often the music of the mystics. Other musical preferences would include the prayer songs of Taizé and other music that helps these people listen more closely to what God is saying to them. Because this type of spirituality attracts those for whom solitude is a better means of experiencing God, there are probably fewer mystics in the organized church than there are other spiritual types, particularly in mainline Protestant congregations. However, their presence is invaluable to those of us who prefer head spirituality, because they help us stretch beyond what we can know about God and into the mysteries of what we cannot know.

A fourth spiritual type is the kingdom spirituality. People with this type of spirituality see their whole lives as their prayer. Social concerns and justice issues top the list for them. They would probably like the hymn "We Shall Overcome," in solidarity with the oppressed and marginalized. Not surprisingly, this group is the least likely to participate in organized institutional religious activities, because they perceive in these congregations a lack of concern about the things they hold most sacred.

Why is noting different spiritual types important? First, it helps us understand better how we relate to God and which activities and disciplines will bring us closer to God. As we contemplate increasing our contact with God, we are more likely to be consistent in our journey if we use means that are comfortable to us, especially if we are new on the journey. Knowing our spiritual preferences enables us to accept ourselves as spiritual beings who relate best to God in a particular way.

Second, noting different spiritual types allows us to see the areas in which we might stretch in order to experience a fuller, more integrated picture of God. God is so much broader than any one person's experience, or God wouldn't be God. Testing new ways of encountering our Creator broadens our own experience and helps us appreciate other people's experiences of God. If you tend to experience God with a head spirituality, a quiet retreat for contemplation will increase your ability to listen to God in the midst of your busy life. If heart spirituality is more comfortable for you, some experience helping poor people—such as a week-long mission trip into the poor counties of Appalachia, or tutoring a low-income child in math every week—would expand your appreciation for those whom God has special affection for, those on the margins of our society.

Finally, noting different spiritual types enables us to be more understanding and tolerant of other people's spiritualities, especially people whom we have some spiritual leadership over, for example the choirs we direct. It is not at all uncommon for the leadership of a congregation to be seminary-trained, head-spirituality people while the majority of the congregation experiences God primarily with their hearts. This tension often results in the leadership wondering why worship is not reaching people as they hoped it would, and the congregation leaving worship with the vague and unsettling sense of not having experienced God. Appreciating that people experience God in different ways has helped me accept those who express their faith using descriptions such as, "Just ask Jesus to come into your heart." I realize now that they are not intellectual loafers but instead experience a side of God that I missed in all my doctrinal discussions.

An Invitation

God wants to be in relationship with you. If you are already on the journey toward God, I encourage you to keep on the path. If you are new to this journey, I invite you to prayerfully take the first steps. Know that the God who calls you into relationship will not send you anywhere where

God is not already present. God will provide you with all you need for a lasting relationship, including the strength and tools to be active participants in this relationship, and friends to accompany you on the journey.

Questions for Reflection and Discussion

1. Do you remember your first experience of a spiritual nature? What was it like?

2. Describe a time when circumstances challenged your views about God and forced you to reevaluate your beliefs. Did that experience make you stronger or weaker in faith?

3. How would you describe God's relationship to you in relational terms? As a parent? a close friend? a second cousin once removed?

4. What factors have enabled you to develop a relationship with God? What factors have kept you from being in a closer relationship with God?

5. Can you describe your conversion experience? Describe it to the group.

6. Which of the four spiritual types best describes your own spirituality? your choir's spirituality? your church's spirituality?

CHAPTER 3:

The Means of Grace: How Sweet the Sound

T*he means of grace* may seem a highly theological, difficult-to-understand concept. The words themselves are easy enough. *Means* is a way to reach a goal, such as the means to an end. *Grace* is that which we have received from God, the unconditional love God offers to us in spite of our less-than-perfect track record. Grace includes all of the good things we receive from God that we can never earn or repay; it is a gift from God freely given. The means of grace, then, are the ways we tap into the love and grace of God. They include observing the ordinances of God, such as the Lord's Supper, baptism, and public worship, as well as prayer, Christian conferencing, Scripture study, acts of mercy, and fasting or abstinence.

Another term for the means of grace is the *traditional spiritual disciplines*. Those very words sound more like a punishment than ways to encounter and be in relationship with God. Actually, punishment is how many people approach the observance of these disciplines. The disciplines seem to call for denial of one's self, giving up all of the things that we consider fun, taking up our cross. On the surface they do not sound like good things to do.

During seminary I went through the candidacy process to become a diaconal minister. That process included reading Richard Foster's *Celebration of Discipline*. This book on using the spiritual disciplines was required reading for all candidates. When my mentor questioned me about the book, I told her, "Yeah, I read it. But all that spiritual stuff is not for me." (I was especially put off by the idea of fasting.) At the time, it seemed to me to be a good idea for some people (read: people who didn't have their beliefs about God in order) but not for one as intellectually engaged with the whole God thing as I was. Imagine my surprise when I reread the book years later only to discover how astute old Richard had become since I first read it! How easy it is to dismiss something of which we are both wary and almost totally ignorant.

Indeed, understanding and beginning to practice the means of grace is a scary undertaking. We need to remember that our goal is to encounter and be in relationship with the living God. These means are ways in which millions of disciples over hundreds of years have grown in their relationship with God and have become more faithful disciples. The disciplines are not punishments to be endured but practices that enable us to hear God more accurately, love God more devotedly, and follow God more passionately.

What Are the Means of Grace?

The means of grace can be categorized in different ways. Some means are appropriate as general rules of life for all Christians, for example reading and meditating on the Scriptures. Some means, such as Holy Communion and baptism, have been ordained by God through the Scriptures as means to encounter and participate in the presence of God in all ages and for all Christians. Other means will vary according to each person in each generation, for example serving at a shelter for homeless people. The means of grace are spelled out in "The General Rules of The Methodist Church" (*The Book of Discipline of The United Methodist Church—1996*; pages 69–72):

- First, do no harm and avoid evil of all kinds. John Wesley, in his day (when these rules were first written), named several things to avoid, among them drunkenness, taking the Lord's name in vain, slaveholding, not observing the Sabbath, fighting with others, being deceitful in business dealings, borrowing that which you do not intend to return or repay, wearing lots of costly garments, and hoarding treasures here on earth.
- Second, do as much good and as many kinds of good as possible. Here Wesley was referring first to the needs, both physical and spiritual, of others. Then he called all Christians to obedience, denying themselves, taking up their crosses daily. Please note that this idea of taking up a cross is not the current popular notion of having to bear burdens placed upon us by God or others in the name of faithfulness; taking up one's cross is an intentional choosing to pick up and carry a specific load so as to participate in the suffering of Christ.
- Third, attend the ordinances of God. Participate in those things that God has asked all faithful Christians to do, such as public worship of God; prayer; Scripture study, be it reading it, meditating upon it, or hearing it

proclaimed; the Lord's Supper; Christian conversation (Christian conferencing)—fellowship with other believers in order to attend to spiritual growth or conversations that introduce unbelievers to God and what God has done; and fasting or abstinence—temporarily giving up physical sustenance in order to become aware of our dependence on God alone and to remove barriers that may keep us from experiencing God's presence. (Note: While Christian conversation is not explicitly listed in the General Rules, Wesley names it as a means of grace in other writings.)

These means throughout history have enabled Christians to know about and understand more fully the God we worship, as well as to experience the presence of God in our daily lives.

Can God meet us in ways apart from the means of grace? Of course, because God can choose to do whatever God will do. Yet God has chosen throughout history to relate to us primarily through the means of grace. They inform us about who God is through the retelling of the mighty acts of God in history. They enable us to experience God personally through acts of prayer, worship, and service to others. Without the previous experience and understanding of God at work in our world and our lives, how could we differentiate between an encounter with the God of all creation and the god of our own creation?

The Means Are Not the Ends

It is easy to think of the means of grace as a measuring stick of our faithfulness as Christians. If we attend worship regularly, pray daily alone and with our families, do all the good we can, and avoid evil at every turn, then we have somehow made it as Christians. That attitude misses the point entirely. We cannot pray enough, worship enough, do enough good, or avoid enough evil to earn God's love. The grace offered to us has already been given, before or even whether we respond at all. These means are ways in which we are in relationship with the One who created us and loves us. They help us know who the God we worship is, what God has done and will do, and how we can participate in God's mission by living as faithful disciples. The means are not the ends; the end is relationship with love itself, the living God.

How Do You Get to Carnegie Hall? Practice!

If relationship with God is a priority for us, we should regularly practice those actions that will bring about closer relationship. Consider your own musical disciplines. While you may not be a director or keyboard player of concert quality, you certainly had to practice your craft in order to reach the musician's spot in your local church. That practice may have been faithful attendance in the choir of your childhood, learning the joy of singing as well as the discipline it takes to learn a piece of music well enough to present it in worship. You may have studied piano, organ, conducting, or voice in high school or college. Your training may even include advanced degrees in music. Regardless of the depth of your musical background, chances are pretty good that you did not arrive at any degree of proficiency without a lot of practice and study. The goal was the joy of music making; the price was the work that you had to go through—learning scales, key signatures, beat patterns, fingerings, bow markings, or pedaling—in order to be free to enjoy the music making.

I studied both voice and piano while growing up. The degree to which I am skilled at either is directly related to how much discipline I exerted while learning. I took nine years of keyboard lessons, both piano and organ. Today I can play "Come to Jesus" in whole notes, but only with one hand. For a graduate keyboard proficiency exam, I had to play the vocal parts to the "Hallelujah Chorus" from the open score, that is, reading each of the vocal lines separately and playing them simultaneously. I passed the exam by memorizing the music and playing it at half the appropriate tempo. Needless to say, I did not exactly exercise the discipline of practice when it came to keyboard skills. I didn't value practicing piano; so today when someone assumes that because I am a church musician, I can play hymns, I admit with some embarrassment that I cannot.

Now the voice was a different matter entirely. I discovered early on that my vocal range is pretty wide and flexible, allowing me to sing the runs in such soprano arias as "Rejoice Greatly," from *Messiah,* with relative ease. Better than that, singing those runs was really fun. So I practiced them with the abandon of someone truly infatuated with a project. I can still sing those runs today (better than my teacher), but I have to practice them to get myself back in shape to do them. The difference is that I valued learning to sing vocal runs enough that I was willing to practice hard to be able to sing them.

Certainly within your local church music program the truth that discipline is a desired practice is evident. You cannot pull out a brand-new anthem ten minutes before the service and expect the choir to be able to sing it in worship with any degree of comfort or proficiency. A group needs to be able to live with a piece of music for a while, first learning the notes, then knowing the music well enough to get out of the music and into the music making. Only then can the beauty and meaning of the music and what the text is telling us about God come through with clarity and meaning. The same principle applies to the spiritual disciplines: the more carefully and consistently we practice these disciplines, the closer we will be to our goal of a more intimate relationship with God.

Practicing the Spiritual Disciplines: A Methodical Model

John Wesley, the founder of the Methodist movement, is closely associated with the practice of the means of grace. Although he did not coin the phrase, his sermon on the means of grace has become required reading for all wishing to understand his unique, methodical practice of these disciplines in everyday life.

The means of grace had been practiced throughout the ages as ways of encountering and being in relationship with God. The Anglican Church (John Wesley's own church) as well as other denominations understood the means of grace to include those listed earlier. The problem was that few people actually practiced them, Wesley observed. Then a small group of people, convinced of their sin and desiring a closer relationship with God, came to him for guidance. Wesley met with them regularly, prayed with them, and encouraged them to begin faithful practice of the means of grace. The results were the development of Methodist societies, class meetings within the societies, and guidelines that governed the members' common life together—the General Rules. Today United Methodists still hold the General Rules as our official guide for living.

In the General Rules, Wesley laid out a method of discipleship that enabled believers to identify those practices that allow them to live faithful and balanced lives. Wesley identified two types of means of grace: works of mercy (doing all the good you can for God and neighbor, avoiding harming anyone or anything) and works of piety (doing things that will open you to the grace of God, such as public worship, observing the sacraments, private prayer, Bible study, Christian conferencing, fasting). People who wanted to be members of the Methodist society agreed to practice the means laid out in the General Rules.

Among the Rules was the stipulation that society members meet weekly to give an account of their faithfulness. This ensured that the rules were being observed and were kept in proper balance. As an active member in any kind of support group knows, participation in a group where one is lovingly held accountable for one's actions is vital to sticking to the program. The weekly weigh-in at Weight Watchers, the periodical chair-leader or section-leader auditions in a professional musical ensemble, and the regular attendance at twelve-step meetings are essential for those wishing to succeed in the goals of these organizations. The purpose of accountability is not to catch someone failing, because as sinful humans we will all fail in our attempts to be faithful disciples. Rather, the purpose is to provide encouragement and support for keeping one another on the path even when we do fail.

John Wesley knew that faithful observance of these disciplines would keep believers from making two common mistakes: formalism and emotionalism. Wesley viewed the members of his own Anglican Church as being primarily formalists. Many of the church believed, or at least acted as if they believed, that if they attended upon the ordinances of God (observing the sacraments, attending worship, and so forth), they were being faithful Christians. Never mind that they didn't help the poor or that their business practices were unethical. Their theology about God was in line, and that's all that mattered. The Anglican formalist knew about God but had not really experienced God, and did not hold experiencing God as something to be desired. Wesley countered their formalism with the admonition that faith makes itself known by acts of mercy, justice, and piety, not just by worship attendance.

On the other side of the coin but just as mistaken were those who argued that the way to be truly Christian was to experience God emotionally. The Moravians were to Wesley an example of this view of discipleship. They believed that the way to experience the activity of God was to encourage passive waiting on the part of believers; so they would sit quietly and wait for God's action in the midst of them. Their viewpoint was that active participation in the means of grace stifles the work of God rather than helping a person experience it more fully. One problem with this view is that it limits one's understanding of God to what one has personally experienced. God is so much bigger than any one person's experience of God (Thank God!). Another problem with this view is that while one is waiting for the Spirit of God to move within, there are people going hungry for food and for the grace of God. To wait until one feels the stirring of the Holy Spirit is to tempt the human habit of laziness. God does not call us to discipleship because it feels good, for often it does not feel very good to obey God's call. Instead, God calls us to be faithful regardless of how we feel. Wesley would go even further and say that to do acts of mercy, justice, and piety even when we don't feel like it opens the way for God to be at work in us. We become vessels of God's grace to others and for ourselves. The result is that as we practice these acts, they become more and more natural for us. Eventually those things that were at first difficult to do become easier, then comfortable, then so much a part of us that we cannot *not* do them.

So Wesley believed that practicing the means of grace enables people to encounter and be in relationship with God through acts of mercy to others, acts of justice that bring about the Kingdom here on earth, and acts of worship and devotion that help them understand God more fully and grow to be more like God each day. By practicing the means of grace, Christians avoid the formalism that comes from thinking they have God all figured out and in their back pockets, as well as the emotionalism that tempts us to leave all the work to God.

The founding of The Methodist Church was a direct result of the success of the class meetings that John Wesley started. Wesley had no intention of founding a new denomination; indeed, he was an ordained priest in the Anglican Church and remained so until his death. However, the faithfulness of early Methodist society members and the witness of their lives drew many others who were seeking to be more faithful in their Christian walk.

The Means of Grace Today

How much like the Anglican Church and the Moravians we are today! Our formalism and emotionalism may take different forms, but they are still present in The United Methodist Church.

Consider most people's understanding of what it means to be a faithful disciple of Jesus Christ. If you asked people what it means, some might answer, "Believe in your hearts and confess with your lips that Jesus is Lord" (Romans 10:9, adapted). Biblical to be sure, but a little short on details. Others would say that a faithful Christian is someone who attends church regularly (meaning anywhere from weekly to three times a year: Christmas, Easter, and Mother's Day). Still others would argue that it isn't membership or attendance that matters but how people live their lives. So if someone gives a small portion of his income or time to charity, doesn't cheat on her spouse or taxes (unless under extreme duress), and avoids running down and killing that jerk that just pulled out in front of him, this person is worthy of heaven. Easy enough, just not faithful to what Christ calls us to be.

Add to this mix the confusion now rampant after General Conference's statement about the mission of the church. "What exactly does it mean to make disciples of Jesus Christ?" people are asking. Add still more confusion because we live in a country that often values freedom over fidelity. What we have is a serious lack of understanding of and commitment to discipleship as Jesus portrayed it.

If the mission of the church is to make disciples of Jesus Christ, if all of the segments of the church are to be about this mission, and if the means of grace are the ways through which people have encountered God and grown in their discipleship, then why do we in the church not embrace practicing the means of grace as a God-ordained, Spirit-empowered, time-tested way of fulfilling our mission? Can we as spiritual leaders of choirs—who long for our choirs to become places where disciples are formed in the midst of music making—not also practice the means of grace in our personal lives and in our choir rehearsals as ways of helping choir members encounter and be in relationship with God?

Let It Begin With Me

I can hear the question now: "But, I'm new to the faith," or "I'm just a musician. I'm not a pastor. How can I be a spiritual leader?" Certainly an honest and appropriate question.

Let's start with what you already are. If you are the director of a choir, you are a leader—the leader of the choir. You may have a little or lots of musical training. You may be an expert or novice at moving a group toward a common goal. Regardless of your training and skills, you are already a leader in the eyes of those who sing under your direction. The question now is whether you will choose to be a spiritual leader.

Remember the invitation at the end of the last chapter? God wants to be in closer relationship with you. When you intentionally choose to respond to that invitation, you open yourself to the spiritual life. As you grow and learn in that relationship, as you practice the means of grace in your daily life, you will grow to become a more spiritual person. As you use what you have experienced and learned in your planning and direction of the choir, you exercise your spiritual leadership of the choir.

For example, directors who have experienced the power of intercessory prayer will build into the choral rehearsal an opportunity for the choir to pray for others. Those who have wrestled with Scripture in the midst of picking out music for worship will tell the choir their learnings as a way of preparing the choir for worship leadership. They will also invite further reflection from the choir members, as spiritual leaders know they do not have all the answers. Spiritual leaders who are also choir directors will offer times for the choir to worship as a community and to be in service to others apart from worship leadership. They will create a setting in the choral rehearsal where disciples can be made and formed in the midst of the work of making music.

Does it take a seminary degree to be a spiritual leader of a choir? No, just the willingness to be on the journey and invite others to journey with you. Your personal journey will involve the regular practice of the means of grace. Your role as spiritual leader will include the incorporation of the means of grace in the choral setting as a way of introducing and encouraging the spiritual growth of those you lead. The invitation that is open to you is open to all: to be in closer and deeper relationship with God. The means of grace offer us the best way to respond to that invitation, both personally and corporately.

Questions for Reflection and Discussion

1. What is your initial reaction to the terms "means of grace" and "spiritual disciplines"?

2. If John Wesley were to write the General Rules in our time, what do you think he would include under the statement, "First do no harm and avoid evil of all kinds"? What do you think he would include under the statement, "Second, do as much good and as many kinds of good as possible"?

3. Are there practices on Wesley's list of ordinances of God that you would exclude for Christians in our day? Why or why not?

4. What, do you think, are the advantages of a methodical and practiced personal discipleship? What, do you think, are the disadvantages and potential pitfalls?

5. In what ways are you prone to formalism in your religious practices? In what ways are you prone to emotionalism?

6. Which of the spiritual disciplines are you currently practicing? Which do you feel drawn to but have never fully experienced? Which are you reluctant to try?

CHAPTER 4:

"God Is Here": Worship

When I worked as a church musician in the local church, I took Fridays and Saturdays off. I really thought I had the best of both worlds. I would get a full, two-day weekend off, and I would be in church all day Sunday. Those years, I secretly suspected that if I worked a regular Monday-through-Friday job, I wouldn't be nearly as faithful in my church attendance as I was when I was being paid to be there.

I put this suspicion to the test when I moved to Nashville. My work at the General Board of Discipleship requires some weekend work and rare evening meetings, so much of the time it is similar to a Monday-through-Friday job in the secular world. The first weekend I was in town, I was faced with a dilemma: which of the many United Methodist congregations would I visit this week? It occurred to me that I was about to do something I had never done in my life: choose a church home for myself. While growing up I always attended where my father was pastor. Once I entered seminary, I found work as a music director; so I attended worship where I also worked (it's a requirement of the job, you know). Not really knowing what to expect in choosing a church home, I decided to visit a church where a friend of mine was director of music.

I was a little nervous on the way to the church. As I drove, I prayed that I would experience the presence of the living Christ in this worship with people whom I did not know. I entered the sanctuary during the greeting (I got lost on the way there). Then the congregation opened their hymnals to number 100, "God, Whose Love Is Reigning o'er Us." The organ sounded the notes of introduction and I drew a breath to sing the first verse. As the congregation struggled with an unfamiliar hymn, it happened. I can't really explain what or why, but a tremendous feeling washed over me like a warm wave at the beach. Here I was among God's people called United Methodists. These people did not know anything about me, but I was at home. I was there and God was with me. Tears streamed down my face as I sang the familiar, "Alleluia, Alleluia" (I think I was the only one in the congregation who actually knew the hymn).

The worship service itself was unremarkable. I've heard better sermons. Few people spoke to me. The music was very good. The pastor was less than warm when I spoke with him. None of that mattered to me. I left the worship experience knowing that I had worshiped the living God, the One who created me to love, to work, and to worship in God's presence. It was then that I realized that I would not skip worship just because it was no longer "required," for it was worship of God that made the work I do worthwhile, creative, and holy. To miss worship was to cut off the source of strength and peace that sustained me throughout the week. I would attend worship whenever I could, because I could not, not worship.

In the six months that followed, I encountered that same sense of awe and presence whenever I attended worship. I visited early services at a variety of congregations and then drove across town to sing in the choir where a friend directed. Gradually, my professional critical self reemerged, and I became more aware of the many things we as United Methodists do in worship that actually keep people from experiencing God's presence. But I have never forgotten the experience, and when I have the presence of mind to pray again to experience anew God's presence in worship, I am never disappointed. Even during those days when my husband and I were dating and I visited his independent, fundamental Baptist church—where I disagreed strongly with much of what I heard, felt discounted as a woman in ministry, and was generally ignored by the pastor—God came to me with a strong loving presence that helped me see and hear God's words in the midst of all the clatter.

Worship: The Main Thing

Those of us from the Judeo-Christian heritage share that heritage with people all over the world, many of whom have different beliefs and practices. However, we all have one common bond: worship is the main thing we do. Services of worship are the only times in the congregation when the whole assembly is united in a common activity: to remember God's mighty acts and praise God's holy name. Worship is what separates us from other organizations in the world. While civic clubs and groups offer opportunities for fellowship, recreation, small-group study, and service to community, the church places these opportunities within the context of grateful response to what God has done for us. Those people who rarely darken the door of the church do so for worship. Worship is what makes us a people set apart. It is worship that gathers us as a community, feeds us with the Word proclaimed and the common Holy Meal, allows us to express concerns for one another, and sends us out to be Christ for the world.

Those of us who are worship leaders understand the importance of the Sunday-morning (or increasingly other times during the week) worship experience. It is the main entry point for new people into the church. We spend a fair amount of our time planning what that worship will include and who will be involved. We fret over sound systems, adequate parking and nursery facilities, what style of music to use, how to include children, which stories will help people understand the Scripture better. The liturgy, literally "the work of the people," becomes a lot of work for those charged with planning and leading worship on a weekly basis.

Because the worship experience is so important, those of us who lead worship often find it difficult to separate ourselves from the planning and preparation in order to worship. We worry about whether the sopranos will sing the descant flat like they did in rehearsal. We wonder if the congregation will catch the fact that the hymn of preparation is a paraphrase of the Epistle reading, or whether they will merely complain because it is unfamiliar. We try to remember if we reminded the children to sit with their parents after they finish singing the act of praise. Worship is important, and we want to serve God faithfully by planning and leading it as best as we can. However, the strain of leadership sometimes hinders our own worship.

Worship as Means of Grace

The challenge to all who lead worship is to step out of themselves as leader and into the role of worshiper. Worship is a means of grace. In worship we rehearse our relationship to God. We tell again about God's mighty deeds, both throughout history and in our own lives. We experience God's presence through the music and liturgy, through relationships and storytelling, through prayers for one another and sharing the Holy Meal. When we have experienced God's presence strongly, we leave the service feeling much as we do when we have spent time with a cherished friend: loved, empowered, and free to be the best people we can be.

How can the worship leader (choir director or otherwise) fulfill his or her responsibility to the congregation as worship leader and still worship? For me the key is in the attitude and intent of the director. If your desire as you walk into the worship space is to worship God, if you pray for God's presence to be known and felt by you and others present, then you are more likely to be open to manifestations of God in the service and to feel, when you leave, that you have worshiped. When you go into worship distracted by wrong notes, missing choir members, a conflict with another staff person, or a to-do list composed in your head, you will often miss God's presence in the planned as well as the unplanned acts of worship. It's not that God is not present; it's that we are too bothered by non-God things to take note of where God is acting in our midst.

I served a congregation where I had a tough relationship with the pastor. Although I had legitimate complaints about his treatment of me and what I considered his level of competence (or lack thereof), I acted on my frustration by checking out during the sermon. My favorite method was to fantasize about the wonderful job I would be offered soon (that actually did happen). One Sunday in full view of the choir members, I wrote out my grocery list. I didn't realize until well after I had left that congregation that my behavior had done nothing to change the situation or to help me worship; in fact, it had had just the opposite effect. Although I was quick to blame my inability to worship on what I thought were the pastor's poorly-developed, egocentric sermons, in reality I was a coconspirator in the deterioration of my own worship life.

We come into worship in a variety of mental and emotional states and with a myriad of things on our minds. It is impossible for us to check our brains at the door when we enter the sanctuary, and ill-advised even if we could. What we can do is acknowledge our state before God, whatever it is, then offer to God whatever concerns and distractions may keep us from worshiping God in this hour. Then we can pray for a strong and powerful experience of God's presence in the service.

Because we bring to worship our different types of spirituality, those acts and experiences of worship that will aid us in our search for God in worship will vary from person to person. However, Christ has promised to be here among us "where two or three are gathered in my name" (Matthew 18:20). Our prayer is not that God will come and be present, for we trust in God's promise. Rather, our prayer is that we may be open to God's expression in this particular service on this particular day.

Another factor that affects our ability to worship is our willingness to acknowledge that God is the primary actor in worship. Because we wish to honor God with the best we can offer, whether it is our music, sermon, or worship order, it is tempting to slip into the trap of thinking that worship depends solely on our actions. If the choir anthem is perfect (or close), then people will worship. If the story or illustration in the sermon is just right, then people will meet God. Certainly God uses our careful preparation and disciplines of worship planning. When we have done everything possible to plan and prepare for a service, to the point where we are able to let go and allow the Spirit to shape the outcome, then worship becomes more of a possibility. However, worship of God is not dependent upon our action alone; it is our response to what God has done, is doing, and will continue to do.

Finally, you can enhance your own worship life by intentionally seeking out worship experiences in which you are not a worship leader. It may be difficult for you to get a Sunday off to worship in another congregation; however, churches are increasingly offering worship opportunities during the week. If you are drawn by the high liturgy of a formal worship experience, you may want to attend mass in a Catholic church. If you enjoy more informal, contemporary worship, you may want to attend an informal Saturday evening service if one is offered in your area. In large metropolitan areas, some churches offer noon worship services as a respite from the day's work. During the seasons of Advent and Lent, some congregations offer services during the weekday as a way of observing the season. In almost every area there are worship opportunities available for anyone wishing to take part in them. If this is a need in your life, I encourage you to look into possibilities in your area. You will enrich your personal worship life, and you may get some great ideas as well.

Worship and the Choir

If you, as director, sometimes have difficulty worshiping and leading worship at the same time, understand that your choir members often feel the same way. While they may not have the burden of the big picture as you do, they may be distracted by their own worries about the music and worship or about things outside of the church. How can you as spiritual leader of the choir help your choir members worship more effectively? You can model by your own example how to be a worship leader who worships. Talk with the choir about your own understanding of worship. Encourage choir members to tell what helps them experience God more fully in the worship experience. If you attend a worship service in a setting other than your church and would enjoy the company of others, invite your choir members to go with you. As in any relationship, they will be more influenced by what you do in their midst than by what you say to them.

Another way to help the choir worship is to explain to them their role as worship leaders. I have been amazed that many choir members do not define themselves as worship leaders. While choir directors often feel that the role of the choir is that of worship leaders, choir members seem to reserve that title for the pastor, the liturgist or lay reader, the choir director, or the organist.

Some choir members may come with the expectation that they are performing when they sing in worship. They understand their audience to be the congregation, not God—or at least not primarily God. They may display characteristics of singers in nightclubs, wanting applause and feeling inadequate or dissatisfied when they cannot, for whatever reason, "share their gift" (sing for the congregation). It is important to convey to these people that the choir is not *performing in worship* but *leading the congregation's worship*. We sing on behalf of the congregation because God has given us the ability to sing a new song in worship. We want to give God our best, so we select music carefully, prepare it rigorously, and present it prayerfully and joyfully. However, what is ultimately important in worship is God, not the choir. Emphasizing the choir's proper role in worship helps them understand that their own attitude and intent in worship is important. Just as the worship practice of a director is observed and potentially imitated by the choir, so the worship stance of the choir is observed and potentially imitated by the congregation.

Finally, you can build into the choir rehearsal a time of worship. The choir is a community, a family of sorts (some would call it a clique). The community who worships together is stronger and more focused on the task God is calling forth from it. A choir that worships together regularly apart from the weekly corporate worship is more likely to be committed to the task of leading worship and has a clearer understanding of the unique role of music in worship. In addition, the byproducts of a stronger family relationship within the choir will help it become a more inviting and nurturing place for the members, as the following story illustrates.

Choir Vespers in Mechanicsville, Virginia

Debi Tyree is an ordained permanent deacon. Like many former diaconal ministers, part of her growth and discernment process for seeking ordination was to think more seriously about her call to ministry and its effect on the congregation she served. She determined that the choir would grow as a faith-forming community if they observed vespers at each rehearsal. She decided to shorten her adult choir rehearsal by fifteen minutes and close the rehearsal with evening prayer. She planned worship using the evening prayer service in *The United Methodist Hymnal* (pages 878–879) and the lectionary Scripture readings for the upcoming Sunday worship. The choir prayed for one another, for the church, and for other concerns in their lives. In order to make the most of the shortened rehearsal time, Debi planned her rehearsals carefully, outlining her rehearsal plan on paper and giving copies of it to the choir. On the back of her rehearsal outline was the order of worship they would observe in their rehearsal that week.

There was some resistance to Debi's change. Some choir members grumbled with the usual, "We've never done it this way before." However, Debi stuck to her belief that worship in the choir is a good idea, and she waited for God to work within that worship. The grumbling stopped after about six months, and choir members began to anticipate the worship experience each rehearsal.

Some months later, a choir member fell ill with a long-term, terminal illness. The member could no longer participate in this community he had been a part of for so long. One evening as the group was praying for this member, someone had an idea: "How about if each of us agrees to contact Joe in some way—a card, a visit, or a phone call—on the same day as our choir folder numbers? That way he would feel our support daily even when he cannot be here with us." The choir agreed and began supporting Joe in a new way.

When Debi told me her story, she concluded by saying, "There is no doubt in my mind that the growing concern of the choir for one another and even for matters outside the choir was a direct result of our time of worship and prayer. The idea for the calls and visits came from a choir member, not me. I'm not sure that would have happened before we began worshiping as a choir." God can and does use our offerings of worship in mighty ways.

A Note About Holy Communion

John Wesley considered partaking of Holy Communion the choicest means of grace. As an Anglican, he was present at the Lord's Table each week in worship. However, as the Methodist faith migrated across the Atlantic Ocean, the emphasis on the importance of Holy Communion somehow fell off the boat. There were at least two reasons for this change. The shortage of ordained clergy in the United States necessitated infrequent celebrations of the Holy Meal. In addition, camp meetings and the revival mentality focused on the sermon and the invitation to salvation through Jesus Christ. The early Methodist Church, which was so successful in converting rugged frontier people, carried its frontier model of worship over long after the nation was settled and camp meetings were abandoned for chapels and sanctuaries.

Worship orders in many congregations today still reflect our frontier heritage more than our Wesleyan Methodist roots. In this style of worship, everything that happens before the sermon is preparatory, including all music, prayers, and offering. The sermon is central. The invitation to Christian discipleship is clear. There is a closing hymn, and people are sent home. Not until *The Sacrament of the Lord's Supper: An Alternate Text 1972* (Supplemental Worship Resources 1, The United Methodist Publishing House) did United Methodists begin to reclaim their common heritage and, like many other Christian denominations at that time, return to an order of worship based on that of the early church. That order evolved into what is now The Basic Pattern of Worship (*The United Methodist Hymnal*, page 2), upon which The Service of Word and Table is based. This order provides for weekly celebration of the Eucharist (another name for Holy Communion that literally means thanksgiving). More and more churches are turning to weekly Communion as a means of remembering and participating in God's mighty acts of salvation in Jesus Christ.

On the other hand, many people still regard Holy Communion Sunday as the Sunday to stay home. Why is that? Some say that Holy Communion often lengthens the service (perhaps because preachers insist that the people still expect a full-length sermon). So maybe people are reluctant to stay longer in worship; after all, we have to beat the Baptists to the local restaurants. People who feel this way may use Communion Sunday as a convenient excuse to sleep in and have a day off.

Some people argue that they do not feel worthy to receive Holy Communion. There is a misunderstanding that we somehow have to be more holy—confessing all of our sins, known and unknown, reconciled to all from whom we are estranged—before we can come to the Table. The prayers of the old ritual emphasize this belief:

> We acknowledge and bewail our manifold sins and wickedness. . . .
> We are not worthy
> so much as to gather up the crumbs under thy table.

(From "A Service of Word and Table IV," *The United Methodist Hymnal*. Copyright © 1957 Board of Publication, Evangelical United Brethren Church; © 1964, 1965, 1989 The United Methodist Publishing House; pages 26 and 30. Used by permission.)

For some reason, some people focus on those words rather than the ones that follow them:

But thou art the same Lord,
  whose property is always to have mercy.

("A Service of Word and Table IV," *The United Methodist Hymnal*; page 30.)

Certainly God wishes us to be more holy, to acknowledge our sin, and to reconcile with others. But if we were to wait until we were worthy before we received God's grace through the elements of bread and wine, we would never receive them. The elements are gifts not because we are *worthy* to receive them but precisely because we are *unworthy* to receive them. The Great Thanksgiving reminds us of all that God has done throughout history—culminating in the great act of salvation through the death and resurrection of Jesus Christ—all because of God's great love for us *as we are.* There is great healing and grace in the Eucharist if people will open themselves to the loving balm it provides, rather than holding it as a reward to be received when they feel ready. For those who will receive it and will free themselves from the fallacy that they have to be whole and healed in order to participate, receiving the bread and wine of Jesus' healing will be a powerful force for good in their lives.

Others say that our "celebration" of Holy Communion is a contradiction in terms. The way in which the church often observes the ritual makes it a deadly and lifeless repetition of words rather than a joyful repetition of God's acts in history, and experience of God's grace here and now. Presiders blandly rush through the lengthy prayers of The Great Thanksgiving. The congregation mumbles the words, "Holy, holy, holy Lord." Songs reflect more a funeral dirge than congregational celebration. Communion becomes more a rite to be endured than a celebration.

Oh, that we could all be like little James when he came to the Communion table. James was a four-year-old boy in the congregation I served in a suburb of Fort Worth, Texas. James looked like a child from Texas: cowboy boots, tousled blond hair, and a big belt buckle. His parents would take him up to the Communion rail, where they would kneel and he would stand on the cushions. As the pastor came by, she would place a piece of bread in each person's hands, saying different words to the children from those she said to adults. To James she said, "As you eat this bread, remember how much God loves you." James took the piece, which was from a wonderful loaf of homemade sourdough bread, and he looked at it carefully. Then he put it in his mouth and chewed vigorously. The look on his face said either that he had been taught to chew his food a long time, or that he recognized that this was the only snack he was going to receive in this service and might as well make the most of it. After finishing the bread, he took his Communion cup and tossed it back like a cowboy tossing back whiskey at a frontier saloon. Then he let out a satisfied and audible, "Ahhhhhh." I believe that God rejoiced when he saw James receiving the elements as the gifts they were intended to be.

As The United Methodist Church struggles to make its worship more relevant to today's culture, we should take note of a current trend in our more contemporary sister denominations. While we are moving more toward contemporary music and styles of worship, denominations and congregations who have been doing that type of worship for some time are moving toward the Eucharist. Their reason for the shift is one of substance. Leaders in these churches indicate that the contemporary music has made them more relevant in our culture but that their services have lacked substance and content. They see the Eucharist as that substance and content that will center their worship on the identity and nature of God rather than on the needs and inadequacies of a broken culture.

Instead of running from the Eucharist as a time-consuming, energy-draining repetition of lifeless ritual, we would do well to embrace the Eucharist in our efforts to renew our worship and bring healing to those in our midst who are crying out.

Eucharist and the Choir

How can we as choir directors and worship leaders help make the celebration of Holy Communion a means of grace for our choirs and members? As worship planners, we can be more intent on putting the "celebration" back in the celebration. Few musicians would deny the power of music to transform a lifeless spoken liturgy into a living act of praise. There are several musical settings of The Great Thanksgiving that break up the potential monotony of lengthy spoken prayers as well as create a more festive mood for the service. Some settings are as easy as those found in *The United Methodist Hymnal*, including those based on the familiar hymn "Holy, Holy, Holy" (Setting A, pages 17–18) and a call and response setting that asks the congregation to echo the song leader (Setting B, pages 18–20). For more elaborate settings, there are many exciting Mass settings found in music resources for Roman Catholic congregations (see *Gather! Comprehensive*, GIA Publications, 1993) that include a musical setting of the entire Great Thanksgiving prayer (if your pastor is a singer) and may be easily adapted for use in United Methodist congregations.

Invite the presider to consider his or her actions during Communion. The story of God's saving acts in history is a great drama, to be told with energy and movement. If the presider is unfamiliar with what to do, look in the rubrics of *The United Methodist Book of Worship*. The movements accompanying the words of the liturgy are spelled out in each of the services of Word and Table (pages 33–50).

Select with care the hymns to be sung during Communion. The time during which the elements are received by the congregation is one of the few uninterrupted possibilities for congregational singing. Make a list of hymns that the congregation loves to sing, and have the congregation sing these hymns while people receive Communion. Use some meditative hymns that reflect people's needs to be quiet and reflective during Communion, but also select some hymns that reflect the celebratory nature of Communion. Congregational singing during Communion helps to move the Eucharist from a "me-and-Jesus" experience of individual devotion to a corporate act of praise and worship. The hymns during Communion can and should reflect once again the saving acts of God through Christ, moving from Creation through the life, death, and resurrection of Jesus, the coming of the Holy Spirit to the church, and the promise of God's final victory.

If possible, allow the choir members to commune with their families. In many congregations in which the choir sits in the loft up front, choir members do not have the option of receiving Communion with their spouses and children. Making the congregation the primary choir for this time of the service frees choir members to receive the elements when they wish rather than at the beginning or end with the whole choir. If there is a time for prayer at the altar, allow choir members time to pray without them having to move as a group from the altar to the choir loft. This may take some maneuvering on the part of choir members or ushers but could probably be accommodated with a little advance preparation.

When possible, perhaps on retreat or occasionally in rehearsal, receive Communion as a choir. It requires the presence of your pastor, but the experience of Communion with both God and one another would be worth the extra effort by the staff.

Talk with your choir about your understanding of the Eucharist. Your own experiences of healing and wholeness found through receiving the Eucharist may open them up more fully to the presence of God. If you struggle with your own understanding of the Eucharist, talk about that too. Remember that your role of leader does not require you to have all the answers. Being willing to discuss questions and concerns can be a sign of leadership as well.

Worship is the single most important and frequent activity we do as a total community of faith. Worship is far too important to dismiss as something we all already know how to do, and therefore something that needs no attention or that we leave to the ordained members of the family. As spiritual leaders of our choirs, we are charged with attending to our own worship life and the worship lives of our choir members. If we long to be disciples of Jesus and not merely church members, an increased understanding of and participation in worship is a great place to start. We can trust that God is there, waiting for us to open ourselves to the creative presence of the Spirit. Thanks be to God!

Questions for Reflection and Discussion

1. How would you describe your own worship life? How is your worship life affected by your role as worship leader?

2. Would you agree with the statement that worship is the main thing we do as Christians? Why or why not?

3. What external factors keep you from worshiping fully in your congregation? What internal factors hinder your complete worship of God?

4. Do choir members in your church consider themselves worship leaders? What factors have contributed to their understanding of their role in worship?

5. How do you think your choir would respond to incorporating worship services, such as evening prayer, into the choir rehearsal? Why, do you think, would they react in this manner?

6. Would you describe Holy Communion in your congregation as celebration or something other than celebration? What factors have influenced your congregation's experience of the Eucharist?

CHAPTER 5:

"Standing in the Need of Prayer": Prayer

"Sweet hour of prayer! sweet hour of prayer . . ." For many these hymn words by William Walford are of great meaning and sentiment. For me? It just sets up expectations I can't seem to meet. Pray for a full hour? My mind would wander from planning my grocery list to making a note to call and get a hair appointment, if I'm lucky. At worst, I fall asleep—and that happens whether I'm praying in the morning, the middle of the day, or at night, and whether I'm alone or with others.

We have prayer times three times a day at work. These are fifteen-minute services of morning, midday, and evening prayer. I used to attend regularly. One day I was praying with three other women, and—you guessed it—I fell asleep. Only I didn't just nod off quietly. I snored. I woke up feeling amazingly refreshed, completely unaware of what had happened other than a vague memory of some strange mini-dreams. If one of the women hadn't told me what I had done, I never would have known. And when she did, I was totally mortified.

Then my friend lovingly reminded me that prayer is often merely resting in the presence of a loving God. If one falls asleep, is that not a sign of trust in God's steadfast providence and care?

What Is Prayer?

If we were to ask the average Christian what prayer is, what do you suppose the answer would be? "A conversation with God"? "Talking to God"? Or perhaps, "Listening to what God is saying to us"? If most of us were honest, we would admit that we do more talking than we do listening.

We often define prayer too narrowly. We think of prayer as speaking to God using certain prayer words, such as, "Thank you, God, for . . . ," and "Please be with . . . ," and "God, please forgive me for . . . ," and "God, I would really like . . . ." Indeed, this *is* prayer, only it is not the whole of prayer.

Early on we were taught to use specific words and to pray at specific times, such as "God is great, God is good" at meals and "Now I lay me down to sleep" before bed. Later we picked up from somewhere that we could and perhaps should ask God for something we really wanted, such as a pet or a new bicycle. As we grew older and our needs and wants changed, we reacted in response to stressful situations, such as just before a test in school when we knew we hadn't studied as we should have. "God," we breathed in the bathroom stall, "if you'll only let me pass this test, I promise I'll never procrastinate again." Right.

Because we often outgrow prayers we learn in our childhood, or remember how we never did get that puppy, or recall that we may have passed the test but only by a few points, many of us simply give up on prayer as it was taught to us. We never replace those childhood prayers, appropriate for that age but not adulthood, with a life of prayer that reflects a spirit growing in God. Oh, we continue to pray at meals and in church. In times of deep grief we may pray the Lord's Prayer. When asked if God answers prayers, we are tempted to answer with a trite, "Yes, God answers prayers. Sometimes the answer is no." While that is true, prayer is so much deeper than that. Prayer is a deeply personal, complex thing, and we are often content to leave it to the professionals, so to speak.

Leaving prayer to others, or adopting the prayer words and forms of others, can be a sticky prospect. Someone once prayed for me when I was sick with a sinus infection. He closed by saying, "And please heal Anne if it is your will." I was indignant. Why would it not be God's will for me to be healed? Could I not be a better minister for God as a healthy woman than stopped up like a clogged sink? Of course it was God's will that I be healed! It is never God's will for us to be ill; that's why our bodies were created to be such healing machines. Certainly we get sick; and when we are, we can learn reliance on God rather than our own efforts. We must also accept that our physical bodies will one day die. God can teach us much through illness and even death, but God doesn't make us sick in order to do so.

This friend who prayed for me didn't really believe all that he implied (or perhaps that I inferred) from his one sentence. He was praying the way he had been taught, echoing the words of prayers he had heard from others. This example illustrates that many of us, even if we are devout Christians, rely too heavily on past experience of prayer to be willing to branch out into new ways to communicate with God in our prayer lives.

We should remember that prayer is a gift from God and is initiated by God. God created us to be in relationship with God, wired us to want to communicate with God. Although we open ourselves to the Spirit's presence and work through prayer, it is God's hidden action within us that prompts us to such openness. Like all the means of grace, prayer comes from God first, and we respond to the gift as we feel led.

How Does Prayer Work?

The question itself may be completely inappropriate (as was pointed out to me by a member of my Sunday school class when I raised the question). Still, it is a common question. Prayer is one of the great mysteries of the faith. Many people say they believe fervently in it and pray regularly but have no recollection of any specific prayer having been answered or do not even anticipate a clear answer from God. We hear about others who receive answers to prayers, but we are afraid that these people are misguided at best, deluded and superstitious at worst. We have many questions about how prayer works. If God knows all about us—our needs, wishes, concerns, sins, desires—before we even speak, then what is the purpose of conversation with God? If God knows all about everything—the famine in Korea; violence in the Middle East and on the streets of our cities; the sins of racism, sexism, and other "-isms"—does God need for us to express our concern for these things in order for God to actively do something about them? These are big questions with no easy answers.

One short answer is, Yes, God does already know us. We don't have to tell God about our inner hearts for God to know us. But, if we remember that God wants to be in relationship with us, the need for the conversation is clearer. It reminds me of the couple who had been married for thirty years. The wife said to her husband, "Why don't you ever tell me you love me?" to which he replied, "I told you once. If I change my mind, I'll let you know." Good relationships cannot stand on a conversation held thirty years ago. They require time, attention, and communication. Prayer is a primary way in which we and God communicate with each other.

Another short answer is, No, God doesn't need us to direct God's attention toward those things that concern us, nor does God need us to tell God where, how, and whether to intervene graciously. If God needed us to direct God's attention to the evil in this world, we would be more moral than God, an idea I cannot accept. Why, then, do we pray? I have to believe that when we pray for ourselves and others, we open ourselves up to the creative, loving spirit of God to work good in this world. When we pray for others, do we not step outside ourselves and see the world as God sees it? Are we not more open to choices that work for good rather than for evil? Are we not more inclined to help someone in need rather than to focus solely on our own needs? Do we then not also participate in the life-giving energy directed toward the good in all situations, whether or not we have any personal contact with those situations?

I don't really know how prayers of intercession work. I just know that they do. I have experienced healing in profound ways when others have prayed for me. I have seen others open more fully to the gentle massaging of the spirit that God offers when they have been prayed for. When we pray for others, we help create a space where something Godly can happen. We participate in the coming of the Kingdom here on earth.

When we pray, we set up opportunities—for God to communicate with us in fuller ways, for us to know God better, for us to participate in God's work here on earth, and for us to be Christ for other people. It's a mystery, to be sure, but one I'll gladly participate in without needing to know *how* it works, just knowing that it *does* work.

Many Prayers, one Spirit

There are many different forms of prayer—so many, in fact, that I am reluctant to start listing them for fear of leaving out a significant form from ignorance or forgetfulness. So, I'll ask forgiveness in advance and plunge ahead. There are also many, many books on prayer and ways to pray, some of which are listed in the bibliography. I encourage you to find one and learn more about prayer as you feel prompted.

Prayer as Conversation

Perhaps this is the most common and comfortable of all prayer forms. We find a place where we can be alone—or if in the midst of others, a place where we can concentrate—and we have a conversation with God. We tell God about the good things that have happened to us, and we give thanks. We tell God our concerns and anxieties, sometimes asking for help with a particular problem, sometimes merely offering the problem to God for safe keeping so that we can concentrate on other things. We name those people who are dear to us, asking for God's loving care to be felt by them in whatever situation they find themselves in. We lift up other concerns for people we don't even know, such as the starving children of the world, or our President and Congress. We ask for guidance for the day or hour or a given situation. We entrust our lives once again into God's loving hands.

We also listen. We wait expectantly for God's still, small voice to offer a word of guidance, of assurance, and sometimes of admonishment. And sometimes we hear the voice. It may sound a lot like our inner voice, like the one we use to have conversations in our head. Or it may sound just a little different. However it sounds, it will be loving and truthful, even when it admonishes us.

During Advent several years ago, I slipped gratefully into bed after a long day of rehearsals and other preparation for Christmas. I began a rather perfunctory prayer in my head, thanking God for the day in all its fullness. I added that I couldn't have gotten through it without God, and I heard a sudden, unexpected response. "You don't really mean that," sounded in my head. It was as clear as if someone had been in the room with me. The voice was quick and sure, but also laughing just a little, although not at me; it was more like whoever said it was laughing at an inside joke. "You don't really mean that," it repeated. I realized that the voice was right. I didn't really mean it. I had been content to steam ahead under my own power all day long, and secretly I was satisfied that *I* had done everything that I had done. There was absolutely no truth in my pious prayer acknowledging God as the source of my ability to accomplish what I had. The voice simply reminded me to be more reliant upon God's strength rather than my own (and to be more truthful in my praying!). I have no doubt that the voice was that of God, gently prodding me from self-satisfied piety and falsehood to genuine humility, from surface gratitude to real thanksgiving.

We can hear the voice of God speaking if we listen carefully. It will not always, or even often, be the audible voice I heard (I haven't heard that same voice since then). It may be our inner voice we hear or the voice of God through a trusted friend or spiritual mentor. The more we are willing to stop and listen, the more we will hear.

How can we discern what is God's voice and what is just our own (or someone else's) agenda making a case for itself? It's important to ask the question, even if the answer isn't always easy. A few tests are simple: for one, God will never tell you to do something to harm yourself or another person. If you are hearing a voice telling you to harm someone or yourself, stop reading right now and find some professional help. God's voice is always loving, even if the message is one of admonishment. If you hear a voice telling you what a terrible person you are for doing or not doing something, that is not the voice of God. God's voice leads us to growth, new life, and that which is good for us, even when that process may be at times painful. But God's voice never devalues us or discounts us as created and loved children of God. A call from God will be affirmed by the community of faith, so testing a possible word from God within that community is also a powerful tool for discernment. Talking with a trusted friend, a mentor, or a group that you are a part of—such as a Bible study, prayer group, or Sunday school class—are ways of seeking affirmation from the community.

When all else fails, time is often an appropriate and helpful test. When I applied for the position at the General Board of Discipleship, I prayed fervently for God's will to be done rather than my own. Many times I was convinced that God would take the decision out of my hands by someone else getting this job. As the interview process continued, I realized that I might have to make a decision. On the one hand, I truly believed that I could do the job. On the other hand, I loved where I was working and didn't really want to move. I was afraid that my motives for moving would be self-serving, motives such as more money or prestige rather than how and where I could serve God best. I came to realize that I would be serving God in either place, and that either decision could easily be God's will. That realization helped me relax somewhat, but the decision was still there. I finally merely listened to my inner voice over a period of time. My internal compass did a flip-flop every day, or so it seemed. One day I was ready to move. The next I was convinced I should stay. I stayed calm and kept listening. Fairly soon, I began to have two days at a time when I thought that moving was a pretty good idea, and one day when I thought I should stay. Eventually the days stretched into three-to-one and four-to-one in favor of the move. I was offered the job and moved two months later.

Could I have been mistaken about God's will for me in this situation? Absolutely, no matter how hard I tried to empty myself of self-centered motives. However, would and could God have used me in the event that I had misread the signs? Absolutely, and God does so every time I mistake my will for God's. Regular conversation with God does not keep me from making mistakes. Instead, it helps me to make better, more godlike decisions in everyday life, and to recover more quickly when I do make a mistake.

Prayer as Meditation

When I think of meditation, I picture limber people in yoga positions humming low, guttural tones. Certainly this is one form of meditation; but for those of us who can't quite put our bodies into unusual positions, there are other options.

In the western culture, we are uncomfortable with sitting and apparently doing nothing. A familiar cliché is, Don't just sit there; do something! Indeed, much of our lack of success with prayer might come from our desire to do something rather than just to be in the presence of God. A saying that might better reflect the nature of meditation or contemplative prayer is the reverse: Don't just do something; sit there! Sitting in the presence of the One who loves us and wants to be with us is a sure sign of our love for God and our desire to participate in that relationship. One author likened it to the experience of new parents, who can sit for hours doing nothing more than marveling in the very presence of their newborn child. When we create time and space to sit in the presence of God—not talking, not even listening, but just being—we open ourselves to new and wonderful ways to experience God.

M. Scott Peck talks about his personal prayer life in *Further Along the Road Less Traveled* (Touchstone Books, 1998). He prays three times a day, although only a few minutes of that time are spent in what most people would understand as prayer. The rest of the time, he sits and looks at his day through the eyes of the "objective Other." He plans his day and then asks God to examine it and prioritize the activities. Later in the day, he looks back over the events, notes those times where he saw God at work and offers thanks, and asks for further guidance for the days to come. He says that he has found God to be the best time-efficiency expert in the universe. Those of us who claim not to have time to pray would do well to hear Peck's experience and reexamine our own priorities.

There are several different forms of contemplative or meditative prayer. A way to begin such a prayer experience is to use a breath prayer. In using a breath prayer, focus on a specific phrase, either your name for God (such as Gracious God, or Holy One, or Heavenly Father) or some message you need to hear from God (such as, "Be still and know that I am God," or "Peace, be still."). As you breathe, say a part of the phrase each time you inhale and exhale. Repeat the phrase until your being is calmed and resting in the presence of God. As other thoughts intrude on your prayer time, acknowledge them and offer them to God for the time you are praying. You can take them back after your prayer time if you wish, or leave them with God. The breath prayer is a wonderful way to calm your thoughts and focus your mind and heart on God. The breath prayer can also be used with any other rhythmic activity, such as walking or other exercise.

Another similar prayer experience is the centering prayer. Find a word that helps focus your thoughts on God. Concentrate on that word alone. When other things intrude in your thoughts, acknowledge them and offer them to God, as with the breath prayer, then return to your centering word. Allow the presence of God to fill you during this time of rest and prayer.

Another form of meditative prayer is the imagining prayer. After centering and resting before God, picture the situation you wish to offer before God. If it is a specific need for healing, forgiveness, or reconciliation, picture those people involved and the strife they are feeling. Then picture Christ moving toward them and embracing them, or touching them in the places where they are broken. Then picture the relationship restored, the illness healed, peace found. Thank God for the wonderful gift of healing available to us through the Spirit.

The guided meditation is another form of the imagining prayer. This works best if you are either in a group where a leader is doing the guiding, or familiar enough with the meditation yourself that you can get away from the words and into the meditation. If you are worried or anxious about something, you might seek a guided meditation that uses your imagination to take you to a peaceful place where you can rest in safety and comfort. If you are carrying guilt over a past incident, you might picture yourself carrying that load like a sack of garbage and laying it at the foot of the cross. Imagine that Jesus reaches down and takes the package from you; thus being freed from the load, you are able to kneel at the cross and worship Jesus. Just be careful that you don't take the load back from him!

For those who are frustrated by our prayer life (or lack thereof), who are afraid of saying the wrong words, or who are afraid that their words aren't being heard, contemplative or meditative prayer may provide a new means of being available and attentive to God's presence in their lives.

Prayer in Reading the Scriptures

Perhaps the best way to hear the word of God is to study the Bible. Within the stories contained there we can see the progression of how God's people have understood—and misunderstood—their relationship to God. From the stories of the Creation, through the praise and laments of the Psalms, to the life, death, and resurrection of Jesus, the birth of the church, and the promise of God's eternal reign, we see our own faith story being acted out.

Certainly Bible study is not unfamiliar to most of us. If we are church musicians who select music with care to convey the Scripture passages within worship, we have to spend a great deal of our planning and preparation in Scripture study, which we'll discuss further in another chapter.

Praying the Scriptures is a different matter entirely. Praying the Scriptures involves not only gleaning what God is saying in passages but also actually seeing ourselves and our circumstances within the pages of the Bible.

If you have a problem with offering the whole of your emotional range to God, then look at the Psalms. There are psalms of praise to God, psalms that extol God's faithfulness to God's people, and psalms that call all of creation to worship God. But as you look closer, you will also notice that there are psalms of lament, in which the psalmist cries out to God, who seems to have forsaken him. Indeed, even Jesus prayed Psalm 22 as he died on the cross: "My God, my God, why have you forsaken me?" Praying the Psalms allows us to hold nothing back from God. God is big enough to take our anger and fear, our confusion and ambivalence.

Another way to pray the Scriptures is to picture yourself in the middle of a particular passage. Center yourself using a breath prayer or another method. Read the Scripture story you wish to pray until you are familiar with it. A good story to use might be the healing of Jairus's daughter (Mark 5:22-43). Pray that God might place you somewhere within the story. Then in your mind's eye, watch the story unfold. See the events occur before you. What part are you playing? Are you the father desperately seeking healing for his daughter? Are you the woman of great faith who reached out and touched Jesus' robe? Are you the young daughter, dead but brought back to life through Jesus' touch? Are you ruler of the synagogue, or one of the disciples, or an interested but detached bystander? Are you Jesus, bringing life to a lifeless body? Hear what God has in store for you as you participate in the story. When you finish, ask God to teach you what lessons you need to learn from this experience, and thank God for the opportunity to live this passage.

Prayer in Singing and Moving

"Those who sing pray twice," to paraphrase Saint Augustine. Certainly we church musicians understand the character of music to be a powerful vehicle for prayer. Perhaps no contemporary form of music better illustrates this power than the music from the Taizé community in France. Started as a monastic community that offered safe haven for those fleeing the Nazis, Taizé has become an international center for prayer, drawing thousands of people from all over the world each year. It is best known for its unique form of music, the Taizé chorus or song prayer. These brief choruses are in many different languages, styles of music, and tempos. Some involve a repeated *ostinato*, or short phrase sung repeatedly. Some include solo verses sung over the ostinatos. They are accompanied by various instruments or sung a cappella. These choruses are repeated as the Spirit leads the gathered assembly. A song leader or cantor starts the singing, and the song keeps going, with people singing parts as they feel led until the song dies away. There are several examples of Taizé choruses in *The United Methodist Hymnal*, including "Jesus, Remember Me" (488), "Gloria, Gloria" (72), "Prepare the Way of the Lord" (207), and "Eat This Bread" (628). These songs provide a wonderful musical way to offer our prayers to God.

We can also pray with our bodies. Moving with dance, sign language, or simple arm movements can help us experience prayer as a total body experience. For example, the Hopi Indian text, "Now I walk in beauty, beauty is before me, beauty is behind me, above and below me," can be set in a simple circle dance. On the first phrase, walk to the rhythm of the words. On the second phrase, bring your arms out in front of you. Slowly swing your arms behind you for the third phrase, and above and below you for the last phrase. You don't even have to say the words of the prayer to pray with your movements. The signs for the words to "Spirit of the Living God" (*The United Methodist Hymnal*, 393) are easy to do and provide a way of connecting the physical words of the prayer to our spiritual bodies. Consult a sign language dictionary for the movements.

Prayer as Journaling

Another way to pray is to record our thoughts and prayers in a journal. Journals can be used for recording dreams; God has spoken to people through dreams throughout history. You might write in your journal a poem or song to God. You can express your deepest fears and longings within these written pages in the same way you might tell a trusted friend. Because God is at work in subtle ways in our inner selves all day long, it is often easier for us to see instances of God's grace at work in our lives over a period of time. As we regularly write down our prayers to God and the answers we receive, we grow more accustomed to seeing God at work in our lives on a daily basis.

I tend to write in my journal more regularly when I am wrestling with a particular problem. I will note the problem and the options I see for myself in detail. I will then wait for God's answer to me—through dreams, conversations with friends, Scripture readings. I record my thoughts and insights gathered through those sources. In time I can see what God's will for me is in a particular situation. Using a journal helps me see the big picture and not just focus on my current needs and problems.

Conversation, meditation, contemplation, reading, talking, listening, singing, writing in a journal, moving, resting in silence. All of these and more are forms of prayer.

Prayer and the Choir

Many choirs use some form of prayer in the rehearsal setting. Most of the time it takes the form of a closing prayer. Prayer concerns can be offered from the group, and then someone—the director or a choir member—can pray on behalf of the group. This use of prayer in the rehearsal is simple and allows input from the choir and the sense that the choir is a community of faith rather than just a musical group. In my former church we had a list of "designated pray-ers" (DP's) who signed up to lead the closing prayer. This practice avoided the awkward silence of no one volunteering to pray or the potential monopoly of the director or another person doing it every week.

Opening and closing a choir rehearsal with prayer is an important step in keeping the focus of our tasks on serving God rather than serving the institutional church, or serving art or performance for its own sake. However, those prayers are just the beginning of a rich and full prayer life in the choir.

As the spiritual leader of the choir, you as director should pray for choir members in your daily prayer times. Depending on the size of your choir, it might be difficult to pray for each member individually every day. However, you can keep in your prayer journal a log of those you pray for each week. Pick five or so choir members each week and pray for them. Listen to God's Spirit prompting you to pray for specific people as well. While you are praying, if someone's face or name comes to your mind, do not assume that your mind is wandering and dismiss that person from your thoughts. Instead, listen quietly for a word from God and pray for that person.

Pray for the mission of the choir and for your work as spiritual leader of the choir. Pray for people whom God may be leading into the music ministry of your church. If you are concerned about numerical growth in the choir, pray for specific people who you feel may have gifts to use for God in the choir. Pray for them before you approach them, that God might open their hearts and minds to new opportunities for service. If you are short on tenors, pray for more tenors or for music that doesn't have difficult tenor parts but will still help your congregation encounter God! In short, offer to God the whole of the choir experience and open your eyes, heart, and mind to what God can do through you in the choir.

In addition to your prayers, ask the choir members to pray for you and for others in the choir. If they know that you are already doing this, many will follow your lead and pray for the choir as well. However, it doesn't hurt to remind them to pray for the choir, for one another, and for the church, that everything in the church might be aligned with God's mission for it and empowered by the Holy Spirit. The following examples demonstrate the power of prayer in the choir.

The choir at St. Timothy United Methodist Church in Houston, Texas, unites each week for a corporate time of prayer for the church and the choir, only they do not meet together to do it. Each Wednesday at noon, the choir members stop whatever they are doing and take five minutes to pray for the church and the choir. They pray for the pastor and staff and for each other. They remember prayer concerns that were raised in the rehearsal the previous week. They lift their service in the choir before God as an offering. Gershom Garcia, the director of the choir, said that the need for regular prayer by and for the choir came from struggles that had beset the church before he came on staff. "Both the pastor and I are relatively new. When I came, the choir was small and a lot of healing needed to happen. A choir member suggested this practice. I feel that it has really strengthened the choir."

The choir also prays at Thursday-evening rehearsals. They open rehearsal with prayer. At the end of rehearsal, the thirty-member choir forms a circle. For fifteen minutes they hold hands and express both concerns and praise reports. Sometimes they stand in silent prayer. Sometimes a choir member feels led to pray for the group, and sometimes Gershom arranges for someone to open and close the group in prayer. Gershom doesn't take credit for what is happening in the choir: "We desire to be open to the work of the Holy Spirit in our presence."

The choir at Plover United Methodist Church in Plover, Wisconsin, is small, almost like a covenant group according to choir director Barbara Kiser. The choir, under her leadership, has an intentional spiritual life together. The group's common prayer life takes several forms. Apart from the opening devotional and prayer time, Barbara tries to remain sensitive to the needs of the choir members. When she senses tension or fatigue, she leads them in breathing exercises and movements to help them regain their focus. She invites them to stand and rub the back of the one standing next to them. She encourages them to shake their arms and legs. While they are doing these activities, she tells them they are rubbing or shaking off the excess baggage of the day, those things that keep them from focusing on the task at hand.

The choir's prayer life extends beyond the boundaries of the choir rehearsal. Every Sunday morning before worship the choir gathers in the church library for prayer. The congregation is invited to join them as they pray for their church and its mission, the mission of the choir, and that they might make a difference in just one life that day. Barbara notes the rewards of such prayer: "It's almost like a miracle that God takes our little group and they sound better than they should." She credits this fact to the spiritual life of the choir. "The music isn't as important as knowing you're doing it for the glory of God. It's just words and music if there's not an inner light that helps convey this to the congregation."

In your rehearsals, experiment with different forms of prayer. For example, if you are using the Taizé chorus "Eat This Bread" as a Communion song, lead the choir in experiencing this song-prayer in the Taizé style. Start singing it and invite them to join you when they feel comfortable. Tell them to sing whatever part they feel led to, and ask them to pray the song as they sing. Let the song continue until the Spirit leads you to end it collectively.

Instead of a traditional closing prayer in which one member speaks for the whole, you might ask the choir to form small groups of four. In these groups, each person takes a turn (or not) praying for the choir, other people in the group, and concerns that were raised. For people unaccustomed to praying out loud in a small group, this may be outside their comfort zone. Be sensitive to that, but also see this as a growing experience.

Expect Something To Happen

Prayer can change lives—our own, our choir members', those of the other people in our church, and indeed those of the whole world. When we trust in the power of the Holy Spirit to work in us and in others through the mysterious work of prayer, we participate in the work of God in strong and practical ways. Lead your choir in the ministry of prayer—then expect something powerful and wonderful to happen.

Questions for Reflection and Discussion

1. Describe your earliest experience with prayer.

2. In what circumstances are you most likely to pray today?

3. How would you describe the relationship between our prayers to God and God's answers to them?

4. If someone asked you how and if prayers "work," what would you answer?

5. Which form of prayer are you most comfortable with? Which forms are more uncomfortable or unfamiliar to you?

6. In what ways are you using prayer in the choir setting today? What other ways of using prayer in the choir may be effective in your situation?

CHAPTER 6:

"Wonderful Words of Life": Scripture Study

There is probably nothing more precious to Christians than the Holy Bible. Through the pages of the Bible we come to know the mighty acts of God throughout history. From the creation of the universe, through the selection of the Israelites as the chosen people, their deliverance from bondage, and God's steadfast faithfulness to them through their bouts of faithfulness and faithlessness; the establishment of the temple; the life, death, and resurrection of Jesus Christ; the birth and spread of the early church; and the promise of God's eternal reign in the fullness of time—all of these events and more are recorded in the pages of this book.

The Bible, however, is much more than a history book. Not only does it tell of God's mighty acts of salvation throughout history, but it also provides a blueprint for how we can participate in that reign, how we can help bring about God's kingdom here on earth now. It not only offers us a guide to who God is but also helps us experience God in this life.

The experiences of the people in the Bible in many ways mirror our own experiences. The Bible is a record of humanity's growing awareness and understanding of, and finally belief in, the God of all creation. The people in the Bible have many of the same problems we do. They cope with life and death, anger and joy, famine and plenty. They are sometimes supremely faithful to God's requirements of them, but often they fail miserably. Yet through it all God remains faithful. If God can use an arrogant man like Samson, or a young teenage girl like Mary, or a Christian-killing extremist like Saul to be God's agents on earth, can God ut also call each of us to live as an agent of grace and justice in our own families and communities?

John Wesley understood the Bible to be the primary source for those wishing to live a life of grace. You may remember in our discussion of the means of grace (Chapter 3) that Wesley fought against the extremes of spiritual formalism and laziness. In Wesley's opinion, careful Scripture study helps avoid both. Those who are tempted to understand God only through their own personal experience ("just me and Jesus") are challenged by the Bible to see God's acts in much bigger terms. Those who are tempted to know all about God but not live a life according to Jesus' teachings are called by the Bible to take up their cross and follow Jesus, a challenge to their complacent head religion. True discipleship involves both knowing God's identity and personally experiencing God's presence on a daily basis.

If you have been a Christian for any length of time, you have probably had at least some exposure to the Bible. You may read it regularly or occasionally; you may know it well or very little. Perhaps you have read it from cover to cover but don't consider yourself an expert on its contents because you haven't had any formal Bible training. Even if you've had some Bible training in the form of an organized group Bible study or a class in school, you may feel less than equipped to interpret some of the Bible's passages. And as a church musician, you probably learned much of the Bible through choral anthems you've sung, played, or directed throughout the years. Think about all of those passages in Isaiah that Handel used in *Messiah*. We might not be able to quote them in speech, but give us a pitch and we can sing those texts for days!

Scripture Study: Scholarly Endeavor or Devotional Reading?

Richard J. Foster, in *Celebration of Discipline* (HarperCollins Publishers, 1988), makes the distinction between Scripture study and devotional reading. Study, he asserts, is the intellectual pursuit of knowledge of a topic. To study the Bible carefully is to understand the origins of the words, the history of the culture in which the words were written, and the reasons the writer may have chosen one word over another. Bible study involves comparing one passage to another to check for similarities and differences. It may mean consulting the original text to see if the translation you are using is an accurate account of the author's intent. Scripture study can be a scholarly, academic endeavor. Those of us who are not biblical scholars are indebted to those people who hear God's call to explore the words of our Holy Book from a critical perspective.

Devotional reading is a different type of activity from Scripture study, according to Foster. To read the Scriptures devotionally is to seek to understand what relevance a particular topic has for our own lives. Thus, we read about Jesus' life not to get a glimpse of life in the Middle East two thousand or so years ago but because we feel a call to follow in Christ's footsteps. To study the Bible is to find out what the Bible says; to read the Bible devotionally is to find out what the Bible says to us.

This distinction is helpful in that it differentiates between two ways of reading the Bible. My own understanding is that as Christians we cannot fully understand what the Bible has to say without practicing both types of Scripture study. Scholarship and biblical criticism help us know the meaning of a specific text, the apparent intent of the author, and the cultural context of a passage of Scripture. Without good biblical scholarship we would miss a great deal of information about the Bible and about God.

However, scholarship is not enough. Just as knowing *about* God is not the same as *knowing* (having a relationship with) God, so knowing about the Bible and what it says and means is not the same as following its teachings on a daily basis. The writer of 2 Timothy knew the value of both: "All scripture is inspired by God and is useful for teaching, for reproof, for correction, and for training in righteousness, so that everyone who belongs to God may be proficient, equipped for every good work" (3:16-17). Scripture study is good, but its purpose is equipping the faithful for righteous living, not just study for the sake of scholarship.

One of my favorite television shows is a medical drama that depicts life in an emergency room. In one episode, a new student was assigned to a weary intern. Eager to have a student under his control to whom he could pass the ugly jobs that had been passed on to him for several years, the intern was dismayed to discover that his M.D./Ph.D.-candidate student was more interested in research on the brain than hands-on patient care. His academic designation meant that he had never actually worked on a patient. In one scene, the student was able to use nothing more than a list of symptoms to easily diagnose a complex lesion on the brain of a man with chronic short-term memory loss. In the next, he had no idea how to take a patient history. This was a fine example of a person with complex knowledge about a field of medicine but no practical experience practicing medicine.

Certainly the same principle applies to Christians. Knowledge about the Bible is not the same as practicing Christianity. Both Scripture study and devotional reading are necessary for a full understanding of the expectations of a Christian.

Personal Scripture Study

For most church musicians, Scripture study is a necessary task for planning and preparing for worship. If the music in worship is to help people know God more intimately and experience God's presence more fully, the church musician must be well acquainted with the Scriptures—both in general and with the specific passages for a given Sunday—so that the music selected will convey those truths in an effective manner. Unlike in other areas of music, in church music the text is primary and the music secondary. Church musicians who wish to be careful worship planners must be actively engaged in Scripture study, both as a personal discipline and as a task of the trade.

Unfortunately, many church musicians focus on one aspect of Scripture study alone or ignore Scripture study altogether. Some church musicians never get beyond Scripture study as a tool for their work, and into Scripture study as a means of grace. After all, there is much work to be done; and if one can use worship planning tools that allow a surface reading of the Scripture with suggestions for service music, why not put the saved time to better use?

For other musicians, Scripture study has little place in selecting music in worship. After all, if the music is pretty and the choir likes it and can sing it, why worry about the text? As long as it mentions God or Jesus, it's appropriate for worship, right? I am reminded of a church in which the choir sang Martin Nystrom's Scripture chorus "As the Deer" during Sunday morning worship. The pastor in this congregation uses the lectionary readings in worship, and the Psalm text on which the song is based was not a reading for the day. I found out later that this anthem was chosen in honor of the opening of deer season. It was suggested by a choir member, and the choir liked the piece, so the director thought, *why not?* Not exactly a liturgical reason for choosing a piece of music for worship.

I have no doubt that people in the congregation enjoyed the anthem. Some may have been moved by it or encountered the text in a new way that week. Certainly God can use even our less-than-best efforts to reach people. I wonder, however, what might have happened if the director had been actively engaged in Scripture study on a personal basis as well as for worship planning. I suspect that the choir would have sung something that reinforced the sermon text for the morning. I also believe that the choir would have had a higher expectation of themselves as worship leaders if they had understood that great care went into the selection of music for worship. The congregation might have sensed the care with which the music was selected and presented. Perhaps the pastor would have connected the song to the sermon, and the whole assembly would have experienced a more cohesive worship experience.

That unity of spirit and intent may happen by accident (but not often) in spite of those who like to wait until the last minute in order to let the Holy Spirit be at work. (My own opinion is that the Holy Spirit can work in advance as well as, if not better than, at the last minute; but that's another discussion.) So, in order for work in ministry to be effective, and a personal relationship with God to be fruitful, ongoing Scripture study as a personal discipline and as a tool for worship planning is vital.

Personal Scripture study can be done in a group or individually, although both is the best alternative. Group Bible studies, such as the DISCIPLE Bible study or lectionary study groups, offer opportunities for study as well as covenant-group support. I've taken DISCIPLE twice, once at the church where I was employed, and more recently at the church where I attend. Both times I was struck by the vast knowledge, insight, and experience one can gain from studying the Bible. I was amazed by the different things individual members saw within the words of the texts. I was moved by watching the growth of class members who had never studied the Bible before, and I learned much from them. I learned from people with whom I totally disagreed. I was supported by a small community of faith who cared about my own joys and struggles. And I learned a lot more about what God is calling me to do and to be.

If no existing Bible study is available to you, consider starting a lectionary study group within your church or community. You may be reading and studying this book in your hands within a covenant community; consider studying the Bible in a covenant community as well. People learn and apply new learnings best when held lovingly accountable in some type of covenant community. Certainly that was John Wesley's preferred method of disciplined living. If you use the lectionary in weekly worship, your study group has the dual advantage of providing both a personal study time and worship preparation time. If you can study the Scripture three or so months in advance, then feedback you receive from other group members may help you decide which music to use in worship.

Even if you do not use the lectionary in worship, studying the lectionary texts as a personal discipline is also a good idea. While studying the lectionary may not be particularly helpful in your worship planning, the lectionary does cover most of the Bible within a three-year span, thus eliminating the possibility of our self-selecting those passages we like and avoiding those that trouble us.

Ways to Study Scripture

Scripture study need not be complicated or academic to be an effective means of grace in our lives. One model suggests a modest but effective way of studying the Bible. First, read aloud the passage you wish to study. After the reading, pause for some silent reflection on the question, What does this reading say to you about God? If you are in a group, discuss your thoughts with others; if you are studying alone, jot those thoughts down in a journal. Then read the passage a second time. If you are studying in a group, have someone else read the passage, preferably someone of the opposite gender of the person who first read the passage. Pause this time to reflect on the question, What does this reading say to you about who you are? After a while, discuss insights with the group or write them down. Read the passage a third time, with a new reader if possible. Pause this last time to think about the question, From this passage, what do you hear God asking you to do and be this week? Again, allow appropriate time for reflection, then discuss your thoughts or write them down.

Such a plan for study is not difficult. It requires little or no knowledge of Hebrew or Greek, or of the cultural norms that were in place at the time the Scripture was written. It needs no teacher or Bible commentary. All it requires is an openness to God's presence and word within the readings, and to whatever resonates within your own soul and the souls of others.

Another way of studying the Scriptures is called *lectio divina* (Latin, meaning divine reading). This is a contemplative Bible study. If you wish to know more about *lectio divina* as a method for studying Scripture, I suggest you read *Soul Feast,* by Marjorie J. Thompson (Westminster John Knox Press, 1995).

Scripture Study in Selecting Music and Planning Worship

Certainly careful Scripture study is necessary for planning worship that effectively conveys the truths of God's word to us. Music can best convey that message if intentional study has gone on before. Not only can the careful selection of worship music enable your worship to be a means of grace for those present, it can and should be a vehicle for forming faith in the choir as you learn the music.

A friend of mine asserts that careful study and anthem selection is the best way to form choir members spiritually. Once the music is chosen, the choir members live with that music in rehearsal and worship presentations for many weeks at a time. If the anthem is one that is used regularly, a lifelong choir member may spend quite a bit of time singing it. The music we choose will shape and mold our singers' faiths whether or not we are intentional about choosing appropriately formational music.

How I have prayed that this would happen in my own choirs! I love Psalm 139, with its assurance of God's presence even when I descend into the various hell-like times of my life. I chose Allen Pote's setting of this anthem to use with my youth choir. As we learned the piece, I told the choir my own understanding of what the psalmist meant by,

> If I ascend to heaven, you are there;
> if I make my bed in Sheol, you are there.
>
> (Psalm 139:8)

I prayed weekly that these young, impressionable youth, who are so prone to extremes in emotions, would internalize the text and learn to trust in God's care even in those hellish times in their lives. Another text that I hoped they would internalize and trust was David Haas's anthem "You Are Mine," a text that reflects Isaiah 43:1:

> Do not fear, for I have redeemed you;
> I have called you by name, you are mine.

I can't think of many texts I would want people to hear and hold dear to their hearts more than these. Because words such as these can lead people to a deeper relationship with God, as spiritual leaders of choirs we much be attentive to the forming nature of the music we select, and do so with careful study and prayer.

In some settings, the task of choosing music for worship is not an individual one. Other musicians are included in the process, some choosing music for singers, others for instrumentalists or service music. In these settings, community Bible study is essential for cohesive, faith-forming worship experiences and choir rehearsals.

When I return to the local church as musician, one of my first priorities will be to begin a lectionary study group with all of the musicians and other worship leaders in the church. We will meet at least monthly (weekly would be preferable). We will study the lectionary reading three months ahead of the date we meet. Each member of the group will be asked to read the selected Scriptures ahead of time and record his or her thoughts. The session will begin with centering prayer, during which we will ask God to open our eyes and hearts to the truths that are to be made known to us in that meeting. If there are concerns that might keep us from being fully present, we will offer those to God as well.

The study will be a roundtable discussion. If there is any background information that is helpful to our discussion, it will be made available; however, the main purpose of the study will be to hear people's thoughts on and reactions to the Scripture texts. Some weeks we may center on the simple questions suggested earlier. Other weeks we may consider other questions: What images come to mind when you read this passage? What do you think God wants us to hear in the passage? How does the passage make you feel? How do you think God wants us to respond? Only after each passage has been discussed will we ask the musical questions: What music (hymns, songs, anthems) comes to mind when you read this Scripture? What music will help the congregation experience these Scriptures in such a way that they make a response to God's call to them? The main purpose of the study will be learning from the Bible as a group. A byproduct of our study will be suggestions for music for a specific Sunday. No one suggestion will be binding on the person responsible for a particular music area. For example, if the organist suggests "The Old Rugged Cross" as a possible hymn, and the person responsible for selecting the hymns prefers "Lift High the Cross," the person responsible for selecting the hymns will have the final say. However, this person should listen carefully to suggestions as if they were from the voice of God. The meeting will end with prayer, both for one another and to commit our future work to God. I believe that a process such as this one would be a growing experience for the worship team as individuals as well as an exciting, creative, and spirit-filled way to plan music in worship.

This process will work in large church settings where there are several musicians on staff. However, it will also work in a small church where those present include the choir director or song leader, the accompanist, the pastor, and anyone else interested in the shape and content of worship.

This process will also work using Scripture lessons other than lectionary readings, but only if the passages are selected early enough to allow ample time for securing music and for proper rehearsal.

Scripture Study and the Choir

Most choir members probably don't come to choir practice to study the Bible. If they are looking for Bible study alone, they might go instead to any number of opportunities for Scripture study available in most communities. However, if most choral music is based on Scripture, and if the purpose of your choir is to make disciples as well as musicians, then Scripture study in the rehearsal is an appropriate way to begin.

Those choir directors who study Scripture as a tool for worship planning and rehearsal preparation often tell their choir their reasons for choosing music, either as a way of introducing the music to the choir or as part of the rehearsal process. Doing so can increase the choir's understanding of a song and enhance their ability to sing it thoughtfully for the congregation. Many times I have chosen an anthem that the choir either didn't like or didn't understand when we first started rehearsing it. (One woman particularly enjoyed drawing sad faces on the music she didn't like!) I found that if I explained the related Scripture text to them, their appreciation of the music was often expanded, and even if they never grew to like it, often they were more open to singing it than they would have been.

A note of caution: the choir director's podium can become the bully pulpit if you are not careful. Because the choir director's role is often that of the "benevolent dictator" and the choir is a captive audience, it is easy to get carried away with our own understanding and insight into a particular Scripture and use too much of the rehearsal time "sharing" that wisdom. Although you may have significant information that will bring the choir closer to God or help them be more effective leaders in worship, be watchful of your own spoken words in the rehearsal. (Watching is one of the general means of grace. It means being vigilant in our self-awareness, particularly in those personal spiritual matters about which we are so easily self-deceived.) One way of being watchful is to write out what you want to tell the choir. After doing so, you may decide that it needs to be said, or that it can be better conveyed in a newsletter article. Another way of watching is to ask a trusted friend in the choir to hold you accountable for the amount of time you spend in the choir rehearsal talking about your study (or faith journey, or even recent workshop experience). This way you can be sure that what you talk about is effective and helpful and not just tolerated by a captive audience.

Another way to avoid excessive conversation by the director is to ask the choir members to discuss their thoughts with one another.

Using Scripture With the Youth Choir

Amy Martin at St. Luke United Methodist Church in Memphis, Tennessee, wanted the youth in her choir to take to heart a particular Scripture passage. The choir was learning "No Longer Strangers," by David Haas. Amy passed index cards to the members of the choir and asked them to write down the words of Jesus in John 15:15: "I do not call you servants any longer, because the servant does not know what the master is doing; but I have called you friends, because I have made known to you everything that I have heard from my Father." Once the choir had written down this verse, she invited them to put the cards in their pockets, purses, backpacks, or school books throughout the coming week. She encouraged them to take out the passage and take comfort from it during the week as they thought of the passage or experienced a time when they felt like strangers rather than friends.

This activity helps the youth internalize a particular Scripture passage, Amy asserts. In addition, writing the passage themselves reinforces the message even more than if they were to only hear it or to read it from cards with the Scripture already printed on them. This is how Amy encourages short daily Scripture study and meditation by her youth choir.

Scripture Is Primary

For Wesley, Scripture was primary. Reason, experience, and tradition were all important; but Scripture came first. For those of us wishing to be faithful disciples and spiritual leaders of other disciples, Scripture study must be primary as well. Scripture study will make us more effective worship planners; and it will strengthen our relationship with God. Whether we hold Scripture as the inerrant Word of God or interpret it through the lens of experience, reason, and tradition, reading it and following its teachings will help us to be more faithful followers of Jesus and better leaders of others who would also follow.

Questions for Reflection and Discussion

1. Has your experience with the Bible been more of study or meditation? Why, do you think, is that the case?

2. How has personal Scripture study enhanced your relationship with God? How has it enabled your work as worship leader?

3. What group Bible studies have been most helpful to you? How do you incorporate group Bible study into your selection of music for worship?

4. How have you used Scripture study in your choir setting? What ways might you incorporate more Scripture study in the choir rehearsal?

5. What benefits come from the choir director discussing with choir members her or his own personal interpretation of a Scripture passage? What pitfalls are inherent in that practice?

CHAPTER 7:

"Blest Be the Tie That Binds": Christian Conferencing

As a member of the Memphis Annual Conference, I have attended more than a few annual conference sessions in my life. Until recently, I don't really remember having Christian conferencing at our conference sessions. We had reports, worship, times for fellowship and getting reacquainted with other delegates, more reports, votes on important issues like equitable salaries and conference mergers, votes on not-so-important issues like where to hold our next meeting, and still more reports.

In September of 1992, Bishop Kenneth Carder moved to Nashville to assume leadership of the Nashville episcopal area. At the June 1993 session of the Memphis Annual Conference, his presence was keenly felt by delegates who gathered in Jackson for the meeting. Rows of theater-like seats at the Jackson Civic Center were replaced by round tables on the floor of the auditorium. Lengthy business days were started with group Bible study led by Bible scholars from United Methodist seminaries. Business sessions began to be accented by table conversations around theological issues and prayer concerning votes that needed to be taken. The whole tone of the conference session was different. Instead of a business meeting with occasional worship experiences that revealed our religious affiliation, we actually had Christian conferencing going on in our meeting. The result was an annual conference session where people experienced God strongly in the worship, in conversations, in study, and yes, even in the business sessions. Delegates left the meeting empowered by a new vision of ministry. Much of that empowerment came from the Christian conferencing that took place.

What Is Christian Conferencing?

Christian conferencing, or Christian conversation, is another of the means of grace that Wesley considered vital for Christian discipleship. It involves telling others what we hear from God and what direction God is leading us, as well as listening to what direction others are hearing from God. It enables us to learn from one another's insights and experience. It creates community where there was once individual believers.

Christian conferencing occurs when people gather as a community to discern God's will for their lives as individuals and as a community. It happens in Sunday school classes, where people discuss the Bible and related issues and what it means to be a Christian in today's society. It happens in confirmation classes and youth groups, where young people enter into and explore a new relationship with God. It happens in study groups, accountability groups, and even some business meetings in which people stop to discern God's will for the community on a particular issue.

Christian conferencing involves not only discernment of God's will but also accountability to God's will as discerned by the group, or actually doing what God is calling for. Determining God's will on a particular issue would be meaningless if the group ignored that will and went another direction.

The role of Christian conversation is valuable in the life of a disciple. Hearing about another person's struggle with faithfulness in prayer gives us strength, hope, and new ideas for coping with our own prayer life. Witnessing another's conversion experience through Bible study may lead us to deeper understandings of the Bible in our own mind and experience. Relying on a group who is concerned about our journey with God and is praying for us will encourage us in times when we struggle. Trusting in a loving community who will gently admonish us when we slip and lovingly call us home when we stray too far into the ways of the world frees us to explore deeply the spiritual life to which we feel called.

In our society, where the individual is held in such high esteem, accountability to a community is not exactly embraced as a sought-after experience. After all, my journey is between God and me and is no one else's business. I can decide what God is calling me to do, and I can follow that call if I want. Our society tends to reward the individual. Those who pull themselves up by their own boot straps receive high praise. Entrepreneurs who buck the system, create their own rules, and succeed wildly (in a monetary sense) are held as examples to be admired and emulated in the business world. Community accountability is out in a society where the individual reigns supreme.

In the reign of God, however, community is held in higher esteem. The individual is certainly valuable, loved, and important; but the community is the ground in which the individual can grow and thrive to become all that God wants her or him to be. Part of the community's role is to nurture the individual. Proper nurture includes feeding and loving an individual; occasionally stretching an individual out of his or her comfort zone into greater knowledge and experience of God; and pruning those qualities that keep the individual from deeper relationship with God. It is in the loving Christian community that such Christian conferencing happens.

"Where two or three are gathered in my name, I am there among them" (Matthew 18:20). Jesus promises that he will be with us when we gather as community in Christ's name. The power of the Christian community is amazing. It is more than just the sum of individuals gathered there and the good ideas, experiences, and insights represented. It is as if God takes those ideas, experiences, and insights and multiplies them exponentially to create something far beyond what any individual could accomplish. This is the power of the Christian community. It is the setting for powerful Christian conversation.

Christian conversation also happens when people share their faith stories with each other. There are few things as compelling or converting as the faith story of one who has been touched and saved by God's loving actions. Hearing others name times in their lives when God's hand was at work helps us examine our own lives with new eyes, looking for the gentle touch of God's hand upon our own stories. We tell our faith stories not because we are bragging about how much God has done for us but because we cannot help but tell that story out of our praise and gratitude.

Sharing faith stories is a lost art for many United Methodist Christians. Many churches have eliminated a time for personal witness or testimony from worship services. Some individuals may think that their own stories are pretty unremarkable when compared with the dramatic conversion of Saul or the deliverance of the Israelites from the hands of Pharaoh. Faith sharing, one may conclude, is the job of the preacher or the Sunday school teacher, not the individual Christian—certainly not me. Some may have tried sharing their faith experiences with a friend or acquaintance only to have the conversation end with uncomfortable silence. Many are reluctant to share faith stories at work because they fear being admonished by supervisors about the separation of church and state, or because they don't want to be thought of as crazy religious fanatics who go door-to-door handing out religious tracts on their time off.

Yet faith sharing is an integral part of the Christian life. It requires being able to note God's saving acts in one's life and convey those acts to one another. It is no surprise that the Great Thanksgiving prayer in the service of Holy Communion is often thought of as a mindless, ritualistic repetition. But this prayer is instead the sharing of our collective faith story: the saving acts of God throughout all of history, beginning with the creation of the world and culminating in the life and work of Jesus. It is vital that churches recover places and times in which faith sharing is encouraged and cultivated so that we might all be able to tell our faith stories, both individual and corporate.

Finally, Christian conferencing involves deep listening. Today, listening is as much a lost art as faith sharing. Instead of directing our whole attention to an individual and his or her words, we are busy thinking up what our witty (or touching, or comforting, or topic-changing) reply will be. In a Christian community, where Christian conversation is taking place, we speak as if Christ were in our midst, participating in our conversation and blessing our communication. We listen to each other with the ears of Christ, receiving words of confession and struggle with loving acceptance, noting potential self-deception with gentle rebuke.

Sometimes there may be no need to respond, but only the need to receive the words offered. Many times in the local church, choir members would come by my office with a gripe, sad story, confession, or problem. Most of the time they were not looking for my problem-solving skills or absolution but merely for a sympathetic, somewhat objective ear to hear their stories. Many times I was tempted to help them solve their problems, only to be reminded by an inner voice that these people did not come seeking my help but seeking my ears. Many times they left feeling as if I had helped them when I had only listened. Sometimes listening deeply, with the ears of Christ, is the best help we can offer anyone. It is a true sign of community, of Christian conferencing.

Examples of Christian Conferencing

The class meetings in Wesley's day embodied Christian conferencing. Their purpose was to act as an accountability group for the members. The General Rules were the guiding principles, and at each weekly meeting members would verbally evaluate how well they had followed these rules the past week. Today, Covenant Discipleship groups provide a similar accountability role for those who choose to participate.

Today there are also other types of accountability groups that meet to support members as they grow and struggle to live a balanced life in this world. Some of the most effective are twelve-step recovery groups, places of support and refuge for those dealing with addictions to alcohol, drugs, food, sex, and other obsessions. The purpose of these groups is growth away from the addiction and toward a relationship with the "God of your understanding." The addict chooses to embrace the steps as his or her general rules for living. They include admitting powerlessness over the addiction, looking to God for the strength to be free from the addiction, recognizing all those hurt by the addictive behavior and asking forgiveness from them, and regularly accounting for one's daily life and activities. The meetings are places where individuals tell their own story and hold themselves accountable within the loving circle of the group. These organizations do not own property or take any public political stands. Their sole purpose is facilitating the recovery of the addict.

Our churches often provide places where Christian conferencing can occur. Any small group has the potential to become a Christian community and a place where significant Christian conversation takes place. A United Methodist Women meeting in which the group discusses a particular book on missions is such a place. A men's prayer breakfast, where the needs of church members and others in the community are lifted up before God and the group, is another example. Sunday school classes, youth groups, even work area meetings—any time a group of Christians gather for work, conversation, or fellowship, Christian conferencing can take place.

However, in those same groups it is possible that Christian conferencing may not take place. Community doesn't just happen when people get together. Many times a large group of people can be in the same room and still be merely a group of individuals rather than a Christian community. When I was in college, my sister and I were invited to a Christmas party of the college-age students in our church. It was in the home of some young women we went to college with, so we attended even though we had not grown up in that city and knew few people. When we walked into the party, conversations were in full swing. We stood near the Christmas tree, taking in the scene. Everywhere were young, attractive college students catching up with high school buddies, laughing, and exchanging stories of college life. When no one spoke to us after several minutes, we walked over to the refreshment table. There we stood for several more minutes. After a while, one of the hostesses came in and greeted us. She said she was glad we were there and introduced us to a friend of hers. "Sally," she said, "these are my preacher's daughters. I never can remember their names." With that she laughed and breezed back into the kitchen. Sally mumbled her hello and left to go talk with friends. We stayed another five minutes, decided we had stayed long enough to be polite, and left the party after fifteen minutes.

This story may be typical of a college Christmas party. Unfortunately, it may also be true in our churches. Many times people enter our doors seeking friendship and community only to be left standing by the tree while we go about our conversations of what color to paint the hallways. Some people come through our doors needing support and help only to discover that we are too busy arguing over what style of music to have in worship. Others may enter the sanctuary hoping to experience the vital, living presence of God only to feel the chilly, superficial greeting of "good morning" as members brush past on the way to Sunday lunch. If churches are to be the communities of faith God called us to be, then we need to recover the sense of Christian conference and community in our walls that other groups in our society seem to understand better than we do.

The early church was this kind of Christian conferencing experience for those who became believers of Christ. Churches today can intentionally offer experiences of community in worship and Sunday school, in Bible study and fellowship, in opportunities for service to others, and in choir.

Christian Conferencing and the Choir

As a small (or not so small) group that meets within the church walls, the choir offers a unique opportunity for Christian conferencing. Although the work of the choir often restricts conversation (try to have an effective rehearsal when people in the various sections are exchanging funny stories from work), planning intentional times for Christian conversation can move the choir rehearsal from a task-oriented group to a Christian formation experience for all who attend.

A way to start is for you as director to share your faith story with the choir. You may have already done so. The value of sharing your own faith with those you are called to lead is immeasurable. These people are looking to you for spiritual leadership, whether consciously or subconsciously. They may need permission from you to be spiritual in the rehearsal. Revealing your faith story makes you more real to them, more like they are. It may make you vulnerable and uncomfortable in front of them at times, but Christian community often begins when we are willing to lower the walls surrounding our own inner selves and allow others to witness the real people we are, not just the persona we show to the world.

Sharing your own faith story could easily be couched in telling why you have chosen a particular anthem. If you are using a setting of Psalm 139, you might tell about a time when you felt God's presence during a period when you felt you were living in hell. If you are singing the hymn "Here I Am, Lord" (*The United Methodist Hymnal*, 593), you might tell of your own sense of God's calling to you. Remember to keep it succinct and to the point. The choir podium is not the therapist's couch or the bully pulpit. The point of this conversation with the choir is not to lift up yourself before them but to praise God for how God has worked in your life.

Don't stop with your own story; the choir members also have stories to tell. Some of them may wish to talk with the entire choir; others may feel more comfortable talking with the person sitting next to them. You can provide opportunities for both of these in the choir setting. If you close rehearsals with some type of evening prayer, you can include a brief time of testimony from a choir member. In some settings, closing the evening with choir devotionals may be more appropriate. Asking choir members to lead those devotionals offers them the chance to share their faith stories with others in the choir. Although some choirs may expect the director to lead this activity, they can be encouraged and nudged into leading this activity themselves. They may only need the green light to do so.

For many in the choir who do not feel comfortable sharing their faith story in front of the whole group, you can offer opportunities for Christian conversations in their seats. If you are singing an anthem arrangement of "When I Survey the Wondrous Cross," by Isaac Watts, at some point in the rehearsal you may ask choir members to turn to their neighbor and tell each other what it means to them to follow the last verse: ". . . love so amazing, so divine, demands my soul, my life, my all" (*The United Methodist Hymnal*, 298). Or as you close rehearsal, you might ask them to exchange a prayer concern with the person sitting next to them. Ask them to covenant to pray for that prayer concern for the coming week, and then conclude with a group prayer.

None of these suggestions need take a lot of time. If a rehearsal is planned carefully and takes these moments of Christian conversation into account, the work of the rehearsal can still be accomplished as well as a time of faith formation for choirs.

Other moments of Christian conferencing may take larger portions of time and may need to be saved for different settings. This is where a choir retreat can be a tremendous blessing. A choir retreat provides a wonderful, time-away, concentrated setting in which a lot of work can be accomplished. I used to introduce all of the Christmas music to the adult choir at an early fall retreat. Such a retreat provides a wonderful chance for the choir members to become Christian community and not just a collection of individual musicians. Community will only be achieved if you intentionally plan for it, balancing times of surface getting acquainted (especially for those new to the choir) with opportunities for deeper discussions. These activities also provide a much-needed break from intense singing that can take place at a longer-than-usual rehearsal. Many good books contain suggestions for group-building exercises; however, in my opinion the best group-building exercises to use with the choir are experiences that relate to the music and mission of the choir.

One such exercise is to develop a choir mission statement. Today many businesses are creating mission statements. This statement describes the goal of the organization and provides a measuring stick by which to judge the organization's performance. The choir can develop a mission statement for themselves. Perhaps there is a professional in your choir with experience in leading groups in developing such a statement. You might suggest that the choir begin with the mission of the church—to make disciples of Jesus Christ—and work from there to describe the specific manner in which the choir will fulfill that mission. Writing a mission statement will help the choir clarify and focus on its true work in the church.

If your choir is large, you may wish to include some small group work in a retreat setting or some other type of longer rehearsal setting. Most directors understand the value of occasional sectional work. Focusing on a vocal line that the basses are struggling with allows undivided attention to a particular part of the anthem outside the whole. The same is true in faith formation. The individual who is reluctant to talk about his or her faith in the large group may find his or her voice in a small group within the choir.

Retreats don't have to be in settings away from the church or to involve an overnight stay. You can organize a retreat in your own church (or perhaps in a neighboring church with a spacious choir room or unique sanctuary). Make it as accessible to the choir members as possible in order to afford the greatest participation. Plan in advance and get the event on choir members' calendars early. Make good use of their time, balancing music rehearsal with times of faith sharing, fun, and fellowship. If you plan and prepare the retreat well, choir members will not only come but will feel that the retreat was time well spent.

A final suggestion for including Christian conferencing in the choir involves accountability. One of the toughest jobs of the choir director is keeping up with where all the members are at a given rehearsal or worship. Some choir members want to be noticed when they miss rehearsal and appreciate a call checking on them. Others don't want to feel pressured to be there every week and may feel uncomfortable if you tell them you miss them. Although you as director may use the words, "We missed you at rehearsal last week," a choir member may hear the probing, guilt-producing question, Why weren't you here? Follow-up is important in any group within the church. Too many times members miss for a while only to realize that nobody seems to have missed them.

Checking on absent choir members is not only the job of the director. Rather, each individual choir member has the job of holding other members lovingly accountable when they are absent. This accountability will happen more readily when the entire choir feels ownership of the mission and ministry of the choir. One way to handle this task is to invite people whose gifts are in the area of nurture to assist you with the task. Another is to inquire during each rehearsal about members who are absent: "Does anyone know where John is this week?" Many times John will have told a friend that he would be out of town on business, and the friend can tell the choir this information at this point. Then the choir can pray for John's travel and business so that he might return safely next week.

Choir Shepherds at Londonderry United Methodist Church

The choir at Londonderry United Methodist Church has sections just like other choirs. However, instead of section leaders, the choir has choir shepherds. The role of the choir shepherd is similar to that of a section leader only much more involved.

Choir shepherds have responsibility for four to five choir members. If the section is large, more shepherds are recruited to assume responsibility. The shepherds function as a normal section leader in that they provide a contact person for members to call if they cannot reach the director. If a member cannot come to rehearsal for whatever reason or would like to express a prayer request, this person calls the shepherd and tells him or her that information. The choir shepherd then relays the information to the director and choir.

Choir shepherds are more than messengers. If a choir member is absent, the shepherd in this person's section calls to find out why. If the member is ill, the shepherd sends a get-well note. The shepherds are even encouraged to send notes to members of the section for no reason at all other than support. They invite their sections to go to activities together outside the rehearsal on a strictly voluntary basis, or to take on special projects at the church as a group. The purpose of these shepherd groups is to foster community within the bigger group of the choir, and the concept is working well.

Bev Mattson, the director of this group, developed this concept of community building and nurture. She uses colorful fliers to give the choir shepherds her ideas for how they can be more effective, and encourages the shepherds to think creatively on their own and discuss their ideas with the other shepherds. She also developed leaflets with suggestions for how the shepherds could be more intentional about sharing their faith. One Lent she suggested in a leaflet that the choir members individually seek out ways to do random acts of kindness, and she included suggestions for possible activities.

The shepherds not only participate in the nurture of their choir as community but also help nurture other choirs. On Valentine's Day, Bev prepared Valentine cards for all the children in the children's choir. At some point during the rehearsal, she passed these cards among the adult choir members and asked them to write a brief personal note to the children while she played instrumental music on the CD player. She then gave the children the Valentine cards at their next rehearsal.

The results of Bev's shepherding program have been quite evident. Her church is made up of members from a wide variety of educational and economic backgrounds. The choir, also reflective of this mix, is intergenerational as well. Some of the older members of the choir have become grandparent figures for a young single mother in the choir. And Bev sees members of the choir who might not have thought of doing so before, now taking the initiative to do good things for others. "The choir is so good to each other," Bev says. "People in it get along because they are treated so well when they are there."

The Choir as Christian Community

In most congregations I know, the choir is one of the strongest communities active in the life of the church. Many choirs are already experiencing Christian conferencing in their rehearsals without naming it as such. That is great. My challenge to you as spiritual leader of your choir is to look at the rehearsal carefully. Are you allowing for times of Christian conversation among the members of the choir? Have you shared your own faith story and provided times for others to share their faith stories? Does the choir have ownership of itself as a community, holding one another accountable for participation and presence?

The choir can be a place for significant Christian conversation, especially if you as leader plan for it to be so.

Questions for Reflection and Discussion

1. In your opinion, what makes a conversation "Christian"?

2. What is your understanding of the role of community in Christian conferencing?

3. How would you define *faith sharing*? Have you had any experiences of sharing your faith with the choir? with congregation members? with total strangers? What happened?

4. What are the benefits to participating in Christian conversation? What are the potential pitfalls one should avoid?

5. Do you think that listening is an important skill for Christians to develop? Why or why not?

6. Does the idea of being in a small group where you will be held accountable for your discipleship appeal to you or frighten you? Why?

7. How do you think members of your choir would react to the opportunity to participate in Christian conversations during the choir rehearsal? Why would they react in this manner?

CHAPTER 8:

"Take Up Thy Cross": Fasting

I have been dreading writing this chapter. I know very little about fasting. I fasted from food once a few years ago. I think I didn't do it very well.

When I plan my work calendar for the year, I always schedule a retreat day each month for my own spiritual growth. In the three years I have been doing this, I have actually taken only a half-day personal retreat. On that day, I decided to fast for the first time in my life. Being a novice, I chose to observe a partial twenty-four-hour fast. I ate dinner one evening, skipped breakfast and lunch the following day, then ate dinner that evening. Although I had planned for a full-day retreat, of course work intervened (I allowed it to intervene), and I began the retreat sometime in late morning. I had an out-of-town meeting that evening, so the retreat ended mid-afternoon.

During my fast, I drank large amounts of my favorite fruit juice; after all, I reasoned, I had to keep up my strength. On the way to the meeting, I spent much of the three-hour drive fantasizing about the gourmet deli sandwich I would eat as soon as I arrived. When I got the sandwich, I ate it in such a hurry that I slopped special sauce on my blouse. Later, I told friends in the meeting about my fast day and felt so good about my efforts.

It was upon later reflection that I realized that I had totally missed the point of fasting. I fasted not because I felt God calling me to do so but as an experiment. I didn't really deny myself, because I overindulged in a beverage that I usually refrain from drinking. I didn't use the time gained from not eating in spiritual pursuits; rather, I spent it obsessing about what I would eat later. I didn't keep my fast private but told about my righteousness to any who would hear it. Indeed, I received my reward that day, and it didn't come from God.

Fasting: A Spiritual Discipline

What's the big deal about fasting after all? It's not in the Ten Commandments. Jesus didn't officially command fasting; in fact, when questioned by the Pharisees about why his disciples didn't fast, he told them that it wasn't appropriate for people to mourn while the bridegroom was present (Matthew 9:15). Fasting, one may reason, was appropriate during other generations; but it is really not necessary or even appropriate in today's world.

Many of us in Protestant churches associate fasting with abuses during the Middle Ages, for example Monks torturing themselves in the name of worshiping God; or we associate fasting with the current Roman Catholic practice of giving up something for Lent. We certainly have a better body image of ourselves than those poor, misguided monks. And what good does it really do to give up chocolate or soft drinks for six weeks? It doesn't help feed the poor or bring me any closer to God. It may help me lose a few pounds, which I could probably afford, but what does it do as a spiritual discipline?

How quick we are to dismiss something we do not really understand and are probably more than a little afraid of. Many of us do not realize that fasting has been a commonly practiced spiritual discipline in every century but our own. Biblical characters such as Moses, David, Esther, Zechariah, and even Jesus himself observed days of fasting. The disciples fasted after Jesus had ascended into heaven. Other church leaders throughout the ages practiced regular fast days. John Wesley called on all Methodists to regularly fast on Wednesdays and Fridays. So important was this observance that he refused to ordain anyone who did not fast on those days.

Fasting in its most literal meaning is abstaining from food in solid or liquid forms for a period of time. The focus of fasting is spiritual. Although some may fast for political gain (as in going on a hunger strike to influence a government's public policy) or to get rid of those pesky unwanted holiday pounds, true fasting is a spiritual discipline. The intended end to fasting is a deeper relationship with and understanding of God, not some worldly end such as political power or physical leanness.

The purpose of fasting, then, is to deny ourselves something we often take for granted so that we may focus on God as the source of all good gifts in our lives, even the very food that we eat. The hunger pangs we experience are reminders of God's gracious gifts in our lives. Hunger becomes a prayer of thanks to God and an acute reminder that there are many in our world who feel these pangs daily. Denying ourselves something so basic as food helps us take the focus away from fulfilling our every want and need, and put the focus on those things that God is calling us to consider and tend to.

Many of us are afraid of fasting. We fear how we will feel physically; we fear how others will perceive us. We may secretly fear that we could easily do without things that seem so important today, and that if we let up even one little bit, someone else may get more than we have or run ahead of us. We are so obsessed with taking care of "number one" that we forget to rely on the One who knows and provides for our every need even before we can name it. In our frantic pursuit of all we want and think we need, we cannot hear the call of God to care for those for whom God has a special love, those who do not have the most basic provisions of life and are on the margins of society.

Fasting can take us out of our own self-absorbed lives into a deeper relationship with God and love for God's people. It can cleanse our insides and sharpen our focus on what God desires for us rather than our own desires for ourselves. It reminds us to spend more time providing for those who cannot provide for themselves.

Fasting From Other Things

Fasting is not only restricted to abstaining from food. We can fast from many activities that keep us from being the people God has called us to be. One year during Lent, I decided to try giving up something. I didn't want to give up food, so I decided to give up speeding. Now, I am not really a speed demon; like many people, I just consistently drive between five and ten miles over the speed limit. So during Lent, I gave up speeding. It was hard for me to do since I often drove with little attention to my speed. I used my brakes more in that six weeks than I had ever used them before. After Lent, I eventually went back to my prior driving habits. However, that time of attention forced me to focus on why I was in such a hurry all the time. Could I not slow down and enjoy the ride? Maybe not a giant spiritual truth, but new insights for me.

The next year I decided to try another "fast." At the church I was serving, I worked with a colleague who was difficult for me to work with, or even to like. He made me uncomfortable, and I didn't think he did a very good job. I began to criticize him in front of other people in the church, usually just close friends whom I trusted. Even though I knew it was wrong to talk about a colleague to church members, I did so as a way of unburdening myself of uncomfortable feelings. That Lent, I decided to give up criticizing this person. Instead, when I felt the desire to criticize, I would pray for him instead. That was even harder than giving up speeding. As I struggled through my desire to criticize him, I began to examine my motives for doing so. Was he really doing a poor job, or did I just not like the way he was doing it? Was it really helpful for me to use my church friends for airing my personal dirty laundry, or was it self-indulgent on my part and harmful to the body of Christ? I never really learned to like this person, and he left the staff shortly after. What the discipline of fasting from criticism taught me was to pray for my enemies (Luke 6:27-28). I discovered that I could accept this man as a child of God and also be free from my sinful acts of harmful criticism. The fasting I experienced in this time was a spiritual experience for me.

A person might fast from many different types of activities. One might abstain from destructive behaviors—to oneself or to important relationships. One might abstain from indulgences in spending or monetary habits. One might choose to turn off the radio or television and listen for the voice of God in the absence of those other distractions. One might refrain from reading literature that does not benefit the soul, or from engaging in conversations that tear down rather than build up, or from saying yes to too many commitments. There are as many ways to fast as there are obsessions that keep us from focusing our time and attention on the God who created and sustains us.

Beginning to Fast

How does one discern those things that one would benefit from abstaining from? Marjorie Thompson suggests a careful process:

> Behind every fitting choice of abstinence lies the question, What do I do to excess? What I do to excess reveals my inordinate desires, my compulsions, the attachments that have control over me. They are precisely the areas of my life that need the freeing lordship of Christ rather than my own abysmally ineffective efforts at control.

Remember that the whole purpose of being a disciple and practicing the means of grace is to be in a deeper, fuller relationship with God. Knowing what things keep us from attending to our relationship with

God, and learning to wean ourselves from those things, are difficult spiritual tasks; however, they are necessary if we desire to have a more meaningful relationship with God.

Another suggestion before choosing to fast is to examine your motives. As with the other means of grace, fasting will be useless as a spiritual exercise if it is attempted for reasons other than relationship with God. If you are trying to take off unwanted pounds or to punish yourself for overindulgence, fasting is unlikely to be a meaningful spiritual experience. You are more likely to be open to God's grace if you genuinely feel God prompting you to go without as a means of self-discipline through which you may focus more clearly on God.

When you decide to try a fast, several excellent resources will help you as you begin the practice. *Celebration of Discipline,* by Richard Foster, and *Soul Feast,* by Marjorie Thompson, (both previously cited) are two particularly helpful ones. Most sources recommend that you begin with short partial fasts, abstaining from solid food for twenty-four hours—for example eating dinner one evening and not eating again until dinner the next evening—and drinking only fruit juices and water. Sources recommend that after you have tried this type of fasting for short periods over several weeks, you can then try a twenty-four-hour normal fast, which eliminates the fruit juices from the day's intake but increases the water. If you discern that God is calling you to longer fasts, please consult these resources or others for guidance.

As you fast, whether it is from food or another substance or an activity, you may wish to keep a journal to record your thoughts. It will be interesting to note how your self-denial draws you closer to God and how often you are tempted to break the fast.

Fasting and the Choir

Of all the means of grace, fasting is the most difficult for me to relate to the choir setting. Fasting is a personal activity. It is difficult to ask others to join us in such an activity, because to do so draws attention to our own practice. And drawing attention to our own practice is, of course, advised against by Jesus (Matthew 6:16-18).

I recommend that if you wish to call the choir to a fast, you do so only after you have had some personal experience with fasting yourself. Only when one can truly empty oneself of self-serving motives for fasting and begin to understand the gifts of fasting can one be free to share that experience with others and call them to join in the journey. As with other spiritual disciplines, the authenticity of your personal experience will speak louder than any eloquent argument that can be read in a book.

There are precedents in history that point to occasional group fasting. Richard Foster notes that a congregation torn by dissent and conflict can be restored and healed through intentional, unified group prayer and fasting. If your choir or congregation is in the midst of such conflict, and if the group discerns that God is calling them to fast and to pray for a solution and an ease of tensions, then fasting may be appropriate action for your choir to take.

Other fasting occasions may also be appropriate. If the choir has covenanted to pray at a particular time during the week, they may also wish to fast for one meal on that day as a part of their prayers. Perhaps they would want to offer the money they would have spent on the meal to hunger outreach projects in the community. Some groups meet for fellowship meals before choir. In these cases the group might occasionally consider using the meal time for group prayers and using the money for the meal to help someone in need. Calling individuals to fast during the preparatory seasons of Advent and Lent will make the feasts of Christmas and Easter all the more joyful for them. Other challenges to fast and pray for specific times and issues may grow out of the choir or come from choir members.

You will probably encounter some discomfort and resistance to the idea of fasting, either from individuals or the group. This is to be expected. Somehow, in our culture people feel much more comfortable giving of their wealth and time than giving up their food, even for a short period of time. If you encounter such resistance, entrust it to God and let it go. Trust that God will work silently in the lives of others and draw them closer to readiness for this new spiritual experience.

If you encounter resistance in yourself, look closely at what keeps you from trying this new spiritual experience. Listen for the voice of God beckoning to you. Offer the possibility to God, and ask that God direct you to God's will for you in this matter. Then watch and expect to receive an answer.

It is unlikely that fasting will play a large, permanent role in choir rehearsals. However, as spiritual leader you are concerned with more than the choral lives of the singers in your choirs. Be open to inner feelings that the Holy Spirit may be calling you to new experiences and stretching you and your choir to broader spiritual adventures. It has worked for countless numbers of disciples before you; God will not let you down.

My Own Challenge

As I was writing this chapter, I was feeling compelled to practice what I was preaching. My normal path is to do something right away, so I thought

I would fast on the day that I wrote the bulk of this chapter. Then I realized that I would be doing so out of a sense of guilt for writing about something that I have some book knowledge of but little personal experience with. So I am praying for God's guidance in this matter. Throughout this day, I have been feeling an urge to fast one day a week during Advent as a spiritual preparation for the coming of Christ and as a guard against the secularizing of the season by our society. Perhaps I will hear that call strongly and decide to do so. As I continue to grow in my own understanding of what it means to be in a deep relationship with God, I trust that I will try many new things. I pray that you will be open to hearing God leading you to new spiritual experiences as well.

Questions for Reflection and Discussion

1. Does the idea of fasting appeal to you or frighten you? Why?

2. Describe how you think fasting enables one to participate in the suffering of Christ.

3. What are the benefits of fasting? What are some pitfalls to avoid?

4. What types of activities or things do you think God might be calling you to abstain from?

5. How might you encourage the choir to fast or abstain as a spiritual discipline? How do you think they would react to your suggestion?

CHAPTER 9:

"Lord, Whose Love Through Humble Service": Acts of Mercy

Okay, so how many times have you heard it or thought it: "My service to God is to sing in the choir." A lofty (no pun intended) and much-appreciated service to be sure, but not exactly what God calls us to in the big picture. After all, when telling the parable of the good Samaritan (Luke 10:25-37), Jesus doesn't conclude the story with, "Go and join the chancel choir." In the parable of the Great Judgment (Matthew 25:31-46) when Jesus returns to judge the nations, he doesn't praise those on his right by saying, "For when I was hungry, you played handbells." When Jesus appears to his disciples again after the Resurrection and gives them the Great Commission (Matthew 28:18-20), he doesn't say, "Go and make choir members of all nations." And when Jesus asks Peter, "Do you love me?" and Peter answers in the affirmative (John 21:15), Jesus doesn't call him to "sing to my sheep." I think you get my point.

Understand that I am not discounting the important ministry of music in the choir. On the contrary, participation in the choir is one of the most time intensive, participatory ministries one can be part of in the church. What other group covenants to meet twice weekly with the main purpose of enhancing the worship experience of the congregation? Choir members are a rare and committed breed of Christians. They may get great seats in worship, but they give up a lot to be there, including family time at home, sitting with their families in church, that last-minute shopping time on Christmas Eve. They are called into service when others may be leaving town to visit relatives. They commit not only to be present in worship but to actually be alert and pay attention lest they miss their cue to stand and sing. Choir members are, for the most part, some of the most committed church members around.

The issue here is not whether singing in the choir is an important act of service. It is. The question is whether it is the only act of service God calls a choir member to. It isn't.

Go and Do Likewise: The Biblical Call to Serve

Acts of mercy represent a rather different category of means of grace. Within the general rules written by John Wesley for the Methodist societies and used by the United Methodist denomination today, acts of mercy are included in the second general rule, which instructs us to do as much good and as many kinds of good as possible. For Wesley, acts of service and mercy to others are means to knowing God and participating in a relationship with God; but they are also a means of participating in the reign of God in that they help transform the world.

Some of the choir directors I have spoken with have told me of the wonderful acts of mercy their choirs do together. More times than not they are referring to the ways the choir members take care of one another. I am very much in favor of this type of nurturing; indeed, the care and feeding of choir members is an important activity that needs to occur often in a choir that is also Christian community. However, it is clear both in the Scriptures and in John Wesley's understanding that acts of mercy extend us out of our close-knit communities (and sometimes our comfort zones) into ministry in and with the world, for the transformation of the world. Remember the fourth part of the primary task as described on page 9? As Christians we are called not only to care for and love one another but also to care for and love the world on Christ's behalf.

In Chapter 7, I described how Christian conferencing had changed our annual conference sessions from weary business meetings into times of worship and spiritual renewal. The other element that had an even greater effect on those sessions was the introduction of acts of mercy during those meetings. On Tuesday afternoon during annual conference, the delegates and guests dispersed to engage in acts of mercy in the community. The youth sponsored an afternoon park fair for some inner-city children. Some of the adults worked in neighborhood centers, sorting donated clothing and cleaning a food pantry. Others worked in a local house-building project for low-income families. Some visited door-to-door, inviting people to neighborhood United Methodist churches. In the evening all of the delegates returned for a highly-charged, spiritual worship event in which we celebrated our common ministry, shared stories and testimonies, and witnessed to the powerful work of God through the various acts of service. These acts of service have literally transformed our conference. When we participate in service to others, the reign of God becomes apparent and the world is transformed.

It is clear throughout the pages of the Bible that service to others is essential to living a godly life. One cannot love God without loving God's people; and God's people include *all* people, especially those who are on the margins of our society.

Old Testament models of acts of mercy include Abraham and Sarah's hospitality to three angels (Genesis 18:1-8), as well as the host of Jewish laws that regarded the care of poor people, widows, orphans, and aliens (Exodus 23:10-11; Leviticus 19:9-10; Deuteronomy 14:28-29; 24:19-21; 26:12-13). Jesus not only talks about service to others but also demonstrates it in his own life. In the parable of the good Samaritan, Jesus clearly indicates that as God's people, we are expected to care for our neighbor, and that our neighbor will most definitely include those who may currently be our worst enemies (Luke 10:25-37). The parable of the Great Judgment indicates that we will be judged not by what we say we believe but by how we act out that belief toward others (Matthew 25:31-46). In the midst of his disciples, Jesus dons a towel and the role of a servant and washes their feet (John 13:1-20), demonstrating that the one who would be first in God's reign must be servant of all.

It is clear that physical as well as spiritual needs must be met by acts of mercy. The letter of James states this core truth boldly: "What good is it, my brothers and sisters, if you say you have faith but do not have works? Can faith save you? If a brother or sister is naked and lacks daily food, and one of you says to them, 'Go in peace; keep warm and eat your fill,' and yet you do not supply their bodily needs, what is the good of that? So faith by itself, if it has no works, is dead" (James 2:14-17). It is not enough to pray for the needs of others or to wish them a healthy life, plenty to eat, shelter, clothing, education, and so forth. As Christians we are called to act in ways that help meet those needs. First John 4:20 cuts to the very core of the issue: "Those who say, 'I love God,' and hate their brothers or sisters, are liars." It's as plain as that.

Jesus reminds us that we will be judged on the way we meet those needs: "Come, you that are blessed by my Father, inherit the kingdom prepared for you from the foundation of the world; for I was hungry and you gave me food, I was thirsty and you gave me something to drink" (Matthew 25:34-35). The criteria for our place in the reign of God is food for the hungry, water for the thirsty, welcome to the stranger, clothing for the naked, nurture to those who are sick and in prison.

Certainly we are also called to meet people's spiritual needs. For many Christians, especially of the United Methodist variety, meeting spiritual needs may be more challenging than meeting physical needs. It is easy to write a check to the homeless shelter or collect canned goods for the local food pantry. It is entirely another thing to spend an evening serving at a local soup kitchen, joining the guests at the table and sharing your faith story with them.

One Sunday evening our church youth group went on a scavenger hunt for canned goods. It was similar to an ordinary scavenger hunt except that we were collecting canned goods for our neighborhood food pantry. Each type of food item received a certain number of points, and the team with the most points at the end of the evening won a small prize. Bonus points were awarded for telling someone about our church and inviting him or her to attend. Still more bonus points were awarded if the person who was invited said he or she would come. When I planned this activity, I doubted that any of the youth would actually attempt this sort of conversation, but I thought it was worth a try. Imagine my surprise when one team came back and said that a member had invited four families to church and that two said they would visit. I think the whole team was startled by the response they received. I'm not sure whether they did it entirely for the points. I suspect that was the main reason; however, I think the youth also learned an important lesson about sharing something about their faith, even if it was merely to ask someone to church.

Statistics indicate that in spite of the church's many attempts to attract newcomers to the faith, a large majority are still drawn to church at the invitation of a friend. I suspect that the friend who lives a balanced, holy life and desires to share what she or he has found is an even greater draw than the most elegant sanctuary, the best-equipped nursery, or even the most magnificent choir.

Many people within our neighborhoods and communities may have most of their physical needs taken care of but may lack spiritual nourishment to feed their souls. Those who have discovered the bread of life in Jesus Christ are called to share that bread with others.

Leading by Example

As spiritual leader of the choir, you are called to lead by example in offering works of mercy for others. This is often a difficult undertaking, not because you lack the desire to serve others but because you already offer service to others as leader of the choir. You may be paid or volunteer, part-time or full-time. Your commitment to the church is already lived out in your service to the church through leadership of the choir. If choir members are to be commended for their service, the director deserves the same if not more commendation; for the director's commitment of time and preparation is greater than that of the choir member.

As important as your work with the choir is, however, it is no substitute for service to others in the name of Jesus. Your gift of leading the choir is from God and certainly should be honored and used in service of God. However, your call to be in ministry to others is a more general call, one that comes from your baptism. The general call of all the baptized is to "serve [Jesus Christ] as your Lord" and "serve as Christ's *representatives* in the world" ("Baptismal Covenant I," *The United Methodist Hymnal*. Copyright © 1976, 1980, 1985, 1989 The United Methodist Publishing House; page 34. Used by permission). At our baptism we vowed to be Christ's representatives in the world, not just in the church. If we are to be faithful to God's call to us, we must participate in regular acts of service in the world.

Service in the world is a call from God and a means to a deeper relationship with God. It also has a restorative quality in our lives. Few things are as spiritual and as physically energizing as helping someone else. Not only does it make us more thankful for what we have, it also helps us put things in better perspective. When we are faced with the lack of food for many of God's children, it gives a different slant to the lack of tenors on a Sunday morning. Working for others in the name of Christ puts back into balance all of the petty things that often threaten to overtake our thoughts and actions, and reorders our lives in a way that is more in keeping with God's path for us.

With the busy lives that we all lead, it is certainly difficult to find time for an extra activity. However, there are ways you can dovetail acts of service with other aspects of your life so that you may gain from both. For example, some businesses support the idea of their employees being in service to the community. They allow a certain number of work hours to be used for community service. Check with the office of human resources where you work for your own company's policy. If no such policy is in place, suggest that your company look into one, and offer to research it for them. Such a policy enables you to be of service at the same time you are on the payroll.

If your company doesn't have such a program, or if you are self-employed or work in your home, you will need to create time in your schedule for service to others. It can be, and perhaps should be, a family activity instead of just a personal one. Service to others is a great way to spend time as a family. Whether you choose to cook and serve a meal together at a homeless shelter, make clothing for the babies of drug-addicted mothers, restock or hand out food in a food pantry, or deliver meals on wheels, your service would benefit your whole family as much as those you are serving. Not only would you teach your children by example the importance of serving others and the value of all God's children, you would also create a sacred family space uninterrupted by phone calls, television, meetings, or homework.

Find time in your life to be in service to those who are on the margins of society. Call your church office or another helping agency and find out what opportunities for service are available in your community. Do it now before you forget. Make a commitment to do something small this week—even if just for an hour. Take your spouse, your children, or a close friend with you. Just do something now. As you do, remember the prayer of Saint Teresa of Avila (16th century):

> Christ has
> No body now on earth but yours;
> No hands but yours;
> No feet but yours;
> Yours are the eyes
> Through which is to look out
> Christ's compassion to the world;
> Yours are the feet
> With which he is to go about
> Doing good;
> Yours are the hands
> With which he is to bless now.

Works of Mercy and the Choir

Your choir may not think of themselves as a ministry group within the church, so it may not have occurred to them to act as a group in works of mercy and service to others. It is your task as spiritual leader of the choir to invite them to think of ways they can be in service to others—both individually and corporately. One way you can do so is to encourage individual acts of mercy by choir members. Many churches have outreach committees that keep track of opportunities for service in the community. You may wish to invite the chairperson of that committee to visit the choir on occasion to keep members informed of ways they can be of service. As you learn of choir members living their faith in acts of mercy, invite them to talk about their experience with the choir as part of a faith-sharing moment. The witness of a person transformed by good works is a much more effective motivator than the spoken invitation.

Your church outreach chairperson may also know of specific activities the choir can do as a group in service to others. The most obvious is to sing or play in a long-term healthcare facility. This is an important ministry that other groups may feel uncomfortable doing because of their lack of musical skills. I would suggest that you leave plenty of time for interaction between the choir and those listening. As nice as the music is, nothing can replace a one-on-one conversation. Don't limit your visits to holiday times. Many hospitals and long-term care facilities are inundated with requests to sing during the holidays, only to be virtually ignored during the rest of the year. Plan to attend regularly and sing whatever worship music you have been preparing.

Don't limit your acts of service as a choir to musical ones. Although music is an important part of who we are, it is not the primary part of our role as disciples. Invite your choir to "adopt" needy children at Christmas. Volunteer to be Salvation Army Santas and collect money for the Salvation Army. Participate as a group in a house-building project such as Habitat for Humanity. The possibilities for service are endless. Be creative; ask your choir members for ideas. Many of them may already be active in community service and may know of ways the choir can serve. Pray that God will lead you to the right opportunities for your group, then keep your eyes and ears open.

Don't limit your acts of mercy to the adult choir. Any children's or youth choir will also benefit from such an outing. Combine the forces of your choirs to create an intergenerational, musical, service extravaganza. Participate in an act of service at your yearly holiday choir party or end-of-year choir party. (I first used the canned goods scavenger hunt as a fun activity for my youth choir Christmas party.) If your youth take an annual summer tour, consider planning a combination music tour and mission trip to sing as well as to be in service to others.

As you plan these acts of service, remember to always honor the people you wish to serve as valuable children of God. Be mindful of their individual dignity and worth; avoid doing anything that discounts them or forces them to accept your acts as charity or as signs of their helplessness. Honoring them as persons of worth is easily as important as taking care of their needs. Treat them as if you were serving Jesus, because that is exactly what you are doing.

Acts of Mercy in Avondale

Avondale United Methodist Church in Jacksonville, Florida, is a mission-minded church, according to music director Mary Wheatley. Although the church is a small one, the members are active in caring for one another and for those in the community. For example, a choir member encountered some financial problems and faced the possibility of having to move from her house after many years. She owned a garage apartment that she rented out to others, and some money-minded choir members suggested that she move from her house into the garage apartment and lease the house instead. They suggested that she could get much more rental income from the house than from the apartment, and this income would allow her to keep her house. She decided to follow their advice. However, the assistance didn't stop there. One weekend some of the choir gathered in her house and helped her move into the apartment. They also repaired the house and prepared it for rental.

This choir's acts of service go beyond the care of choir members. The whole church assists in a program to help feed homeless people. The facility was in need of repair, so the church—including most of the choir—took on the job of painting the kitchen and the eating hall one Saturday. The next day many of the singers were hoarse from inhaling paint fumes, and Mary admits that they didn't sound as good as they normally do. In addition, the soloist was suffering from a sore back after painting the ceiling for hours the day before. Mary told him that they might want to reschedule his solo next time if he has plans to do any painting the day before. In the minds of these Christians their duty is clear, even if the singing has to suffer a little from time to time.

Acts of service within the choir can have the same effect on the corporate body as they do on the individual. Service can reinvigorate the music we sing by giving us a broader understanding of the God to whom, for whom, and about whom we sing. It can help us keep a balance between those things we do for ourselves and those we do for God. And it can make our service in the choir even more meaningful and vital to our lives as faithful disciples.

Questions for Reflection and Discussion

1. Describe your understanding of the difference between acts of mercy and acts of compassion.

2. Do you agree with the idea that all Christians are called to serve in the world apart from their service in the church? Why or why not?

3. How do you currently act upon God's call to you to be an agent of mercy in the world?

4. What works of mercy is your choir currently participating in outside of your local church?

5. Do you agree that an active life of service apart from the local church would have a positive effect on the choir's ability to lead worship more effectively? Why or why not?

6. How do you think your choir would respond to the call to service beyond the choir and the local church? Why, do you think, would they respond in this manner?

CHAPTER 10:

Spiritual Leadership and the Choir

I come from a long line of United Methodist ministers. My father is a United Methodist pastor. My grandfather was a Methodist pastor. My great-grandfather on my mother's side was a Methodist circuit rider, and my great-grandfather on my father's side was a lay preacher as well as a sign painter and farmer.

What is interesting to note about my ancestors is the vast difference in their experiences with and expectations of ministry. The expectations and demands of ministry at the beginning of this century when my great-grandfathers were active involved circuit work instead of an appointment to a single congregation. In addition, preaching was a vocation rather than an occupation; many preachers worked full-time jobs during the week in order to support their families, then preached on the weekends. Compensation was often in the form of food, with hams and live chickens being offered to clergy families in place of salary.

By the time of my father's ministry, expectations and demands of pastors had changed greatly. Many of our clergy had graduate degrees in religion. Many were financially compensated for the amount of education and experience they had acquired. Ministry had become a profession as well as a vocation. With this change came some real benefits for clergy (and their families. It's difficult to raise a family in today's world being paid with hams and chickens!). However, this change also resulted in a thinking shift in the minds of church members. They began to think that ministry is the realm of the professional. *Let the clergy do the ministry,* the thinking went. *After all, that is why we pay them.*

In our day, the expectations of clergy have changed once again. The expectation of clergy in the early twentieth century was to give up hopes of financial security for the sake of spreading the gospel. The expectation of clergy in the middle of the century was to obtain professional knowledge in order to lead the church effectively in ministry. What are the expectations of ministry leaders now? While professional knowledge in areas of leadership is still desired, a new and overriding expectation is keenly present: that leaders in congregations will be *spiritual* leaders, people with authentic, personal experiences of God at work in their lives and evident in their ministry.

The call for church leaders to be spiritual leaders is not merely an expectation of those we serve in our congregations and those we seek to introduce to life with Christ. The call to be spiritual leaders is made clear in our baptism. When we were baptized or confirmed, we covenanted to be "Christ's *representatives* in the world" ("Baptismal Covenant I," *The United Methodist Hymnal*; page 34). As baptized Christians we reaffirm that covenant every time we participate in the baptism of another, when we promise that

> . . . we will proclaim the good news
> and live according to the example of Christ.
>
> ("Baptismal Covenant I," *The United Methodist Hymnal*; page 40.)

Note that our call as baptized Christians is not to gain all the professional knowledge we can but to live and walk as disciples of Jesus Christ our whole lives, to see our whole lives as ministry, and to call others to that same life of discipleship by the example of our lives.

This call to be spiritual leader is relevant for ordained clergy who are appointed to serve our congregations. But it is also expected of the lay leader who is chairing the administrative council, the woman who is organizing outreach ministries for the church, the man who is teaching elementary Sunday school. And it is expected of the one who leads the choir.

Being a Spiritual Leader

Each of us can probably point to a person in our lives who has demonstrated the qualities of spiritual leadership. Although these people's personalities, spiritual gifts, and areas of ministry may be vastly different, they have at least two qualities in common: a deep, personal, authentic relationship with God, evident in the whole of their lives, and the ability and willingness to lead others to and on the journey into a deeper relationship with God.

As a spiritual leader of choirs, your first call is to be in relationship with God. You cannot lead others to a place where you are not going yourself. Imagine that you are driving in an area you have not been in before. Your destination is unfamiliar to you, and you stop to ask for directions. Are you more likely to trust someone who is familiar with the area, who has lived and traveled these roads before, or another stranger on the road with you? Of course you will trust the one who is familiar with the territory and knows the place that you are trying to reach.

Taking the analogy further, assume that the route to the place you are going is complicated. There are some detours on the path, and the markers and signs are hard to read. Are you not even more grateful for the one who not only offers directions to you but also takes the time and energy to lead you there? In the same way, those whom you lead will be more likely to follow you if you are familiar with the path and are a fellow traveler on the journey with them.

If you are the leader of a church choir, the invitation is clear: God through Jesus Christ invites you to be in a deeper relationship with God and to lead others into that relationship as well.

Getting Started

Throughout this book, I have attempted to present the spiritual life in general, and practicing the means of grace in particular, as the best way to go about being a spiritual leader. I hope that in your reading and reflecting on this book, you have thought of ways you can begin your journey or move into a deeper relationship with God. What I offer you now are some suggestions for putting these disciplines to work in your life.

- *Commit to practicing the means of grace in your daily life.*

First, take inventory of what you are already doing. When do you pray? When do you study the Scripture? Do you engage in intentional Christian conferencing, fasting or abstinence, and acts of mercy? Do you worship and partake of the Lord's Supper whenever you are able? Answering these questions will help you see the ways you are currently practicing these disciplines.

Note the areas in which you are not regularly practicing the means of grace. Are you, as the leader of the choir, so caught up in directing that you are unable to worship fully? Do you pray only when there is a crisis or when called upon by your ministry responsibilities? Do you engage in acts of mercy in your community apart from your work in the church? Is your Scripture study limited to the time you spend selecting appropriate anthems for the choir to sing in worship? Have you always considered fasting as irrelevant for modern-day Protestants? What keeps you from doing these things?

After determining which means you are currently practicing and which you are not practicing, listen to what God is calling you to do. Pray with these means in mind. Talk with your family about your desire to practice these disciplines more faithfully. Look for opportunities to practice these disciplines in your daily life. What needs do you see in your community and church? Remember that God will speak through the people and circumstances around you.

As you seek to understand what God is calling you to do, begin to increase your regular practice of these means. Set aside a daily time for prayer and Scripture study, however brief it may be. Be intentional about your full participation in worship. Pray for an opportunity to be in service to someone in need. You do not have to be clear about God's direction for you in order to begin practicing these disciplines on a daily basis.

• *Consider participating in some kind of accountability group.*

Those who participate in twelve-step programs or a weight-loss group such as Weight Watchers know the value of accountability and support. How easy it is to start an exercise program on your own and follow it faithfully for a time, only to drop it after several weeks. It is much easier to be faithful and much more difficult to fall away from a practice if you have another person who is doing the exercise with you and will be affected if you quit. The same is true for spiritual disciplines. Having a group that both supports you and holds you accountable for your spiritual journey will increase your ability to be faithful on the journey.

Covenant Discipleship groups offer a model for accountability groups. Patterned after the Methodist class meetings, these groups offer a structure for those who want to practice the means of grace regularly and to have a group to be accountable with.

You may also wish to participate in a small group that has a specific focus (such as a lectionary study group) but that could also function as a support and accountability group for the members. As well as completing the task or study at hand, you can also introduce the means of grace to the group and ask that you hold one another accountable for regular practice of them.

Remember that the purpose of such a small group is not to make you feel guilty about what you are not doing but to offer support and assistance for what you would like to do. Others cannot judge whether you are being faithful to what you feel called to do; only you can judge your faithfulness. Others can offer suggestions to you and prayer support for you as you struggle to be faithful in the midst of your daily life. Participation in such a group eliminates the isolation and loneliness that often exist in our lives, and gives us a glimpse of the heavenly community to which we all belong.

- *START SMALL.*

Almost everyone has decided to give up something that we enjoy because we feel that it is not healthy for us. We decide to give up chocolate or junk foods entirely so that we might live a more healthy life. Inevitably, unless we have an iron will, the desire to eat these things again overcomes our best intentions and we give in to the temptation. Or, on a more positive note, we may decide to add a vigorous exercise regimen to our daily activities. So we decide to get up an hour earlier and take a stimulating walk or go to the health club every day. This may work for a while, but old patterns of behavior often creep up on us. One day we decide that sleep is more important, or we succumb to an illness or injury that interrupts our new practice. We give up a good idea because we took on too much at once.

God is calling us to be in deeper relationship with God, not to knock ourselves out trying to do it right. God calls us from where we are and invites us to inch a little closer to God today. As you consider what you would like to do to increase your contact with God, start with something small. If you don't currently have a daily devotion, find a brief time in your day that you can spend in prayer and study. Morning may be the best time, or fifteen minutes at lunch, or before you go to bed. Purchase a small devotional guide to help you and a small notebook to record prayer concerns.

Resist the desire to make a lot of changes all at once. Unless you have extraordinary willpower and time and are clear that God is calling you to do so, don't commit simultaneously to a year-long, intensive Bible study, participation in a weekly accountability group, and hour-long daily devotions. When we discover the power of these disciplines, we are often tempted to go overboard. (Anything worth doing is worth overdoing, as the saying goes.) Remember that spiritual disciplines are means to a relationship with God, not ends in themselves.

Finally, don't expect grand and glorious things to happen right away. Right after I wrote the chapter on fasting, I prayed that God would help me understand it better, and I decided to try it on a regular basis for a short period of time. So, I decided to engage in a partial fast once a week during Advent. The first two weeks went pretty well; other than a hunger headache and a small sense of satisfaction, nothing much different occurred. On the third week, the day I chose to fast was marked by the traditional bringing of Christmas cookies to the office. I was sorely tempted by those cookies. I began to argue with myself and with God: *Why am I fasting anyway? I can't really tell any difference in my life. Would it hurt if I had only one cookie—or two?* The answer came slowly but surely: I was not fasting for what I could get out of it but because I believed I heard the call of God to try it. What I felt or did not feel didn't really matter; what mattered was my desire to be obedient to God.

Great rewards will come from a closer relationship with God; however, these rewards are not always the instant gratification we like to experience. More often they are the gradual and sure rewards that come to those who are consistent and faithful. In the same way that fitness comes gradually to those who exercise regularly and consistently, so the rewards of a closer relationship with God will come to those who are faithful and consistent in their spiritual disciplines.

A Promise of Hope

God calls us into deeper relationship. God provides all that we need to participate in that relationship: the means of grace. All we need to do is respond to that invitation by using the tools that God has given us and trusting that God will continue to provide all we need. And we have this promise: "that the one who began a good work among you will bring it to completion by the day of Jesus Christ" (Philippians 1:6).

Questions for Reflection and Discussion

1. In your opinion, how have the expectations of pastors and church members changed in the last several decades, especially with regard to spiritual matters?

2. How do you feel about your call to be a spiritual leader? Are you prepared to accept that role and work toward it, or are you put off by that expectation of you by others?

3. What steps are you willing to take today to begin or continue your relationship with God?

CHAPTER 11:

Spirituality and the Choir: Rehearsal Planning

My guess is that if you have read this far, you are responding in one of two ways. Perhaps this describes you: You hear God calling you to be a spiritual leader of your choir. You begin (or continue) traveling down that intentional road of personal spiritual formation. You were convinced before you read any of this that Christian formation is a task of the choir. You engage in that endeavor in rehearsals when possible, and you are looking for new ways to more intentionally form choir members spiritually through the choir experience.

Or perhaps you are more skeptical: "Don't we as choir directors have enough to do in a choir rehearsal without having to worry about adding something new?" "Oh, I'm all in favor of spiritual disciplines, but my choir would never go for this." As the joke goes, How many United Methodists does it take to change a light bulb? Answer: Who said anything about change? We humans are resistant to change. We don't want to change things unless they are truly broken. And our churches and choirs are working just fine the way they are, thank you very much.

Our churches and choirs may be working just fine, and people are more or less being transformed into disciples because of and in spite of our best efforts. We could continue to do things in the way that we have always done them and trust that God will use our efforts.

Or we can listen and respond to people in our world who are broken and seek healing through a relationship with the living God through Jesus Christ. We can offer them the hope and salvation that we have found in our relationship with God. We can do so in and through the choir experience.

Intentional Christian Formation in the Choir: Both New and Difficult

Leading the choir in such a way that disciples are formed and sent into the world is a difficult task. That I know from experience. But I also know from experience how easy it is to focus on the things that are familiar and comfortable. Rehearsing choir music for Sunday is what we do each week; praying together for the emotional needs of a member happens perhaps less frequently. Picking out and preparing an anthem that reflects God's call to us to care for the least of these is easy and comfortable for us to do; discussing as a choir how we can live out that call faithfully, both individually and as a group, is more difficult and uncomfortable; choosing to spend time off feeding the homeless in a rather dangerous section of town may be close to impossible. Leading music in worship is what we signed up for; leading others through a process of making disciples may be way beyond our comfort zone.

Being a faithful disciple means that we must constantly ask ourselves if what we are doing is what God wants us to do. Watching, one of the general means of grace, is regular self-examination through the eyes of God. In the choir, watching may take the form of asking these questions:

- What is the purpose and mission of this choir? How is that mission connected with the mission of the church (remember the primary task)? Is this what God wants us to do and be?
- How do we fulfill that mission and purpose on a weekly basis?
- What could we do to better fulfill that mission and purpose?

When we answer these questions honestly, we may discover that we are more or less adequately fulfilling the role as provider and leader of music in worship. In some ways our worship role connects us to the church's overall mission. Certainly disciples are made and formed through the worship experience. The worship experience is enriched by carefully prepared and presented music.

However, we must also focus on the rehearsal itself. In what ways are we making and forming disciples in the rehearsal? On a weekly basis the choir spends more time in rehearsal than in worship. Is it not important that we also focus on what spiritual formation happens during rehearsal? It is that focus that I believe deserves our critical attention.

Rehearsal Planning With Formation in Mind

Planning an effective rehearsal requires a great deal of thought and preparation. As you plan choir rehearsals with Christian formation in mind, consider the following suggestions.

• *Pick your music carefully and with formation in mind.*

Certainly the music you select for worship will greatly shape the way you help form the members of your choir. We have already talked about how your own Scripture study will affect what music you select and why. Understanding what spiritual truth you see evident in a particular anthem is a first step.

As you plan how you will teach a particular anthem to the choir, think about how you can introduce the spiritual components as well as the musical aspects. Just as you would think intentionally about how you can teach a particularly difficult rhythmic passage, consider how you can engage the choir's minds and hearts with the theological substance. You may wish to explain why you chose this particular piece of music for a given Scripture passage or seasonal focus. You may also plan to invite choir members to tell one another what a certain line of the text says to them, or to tell an experience they have had that supports the idea. Just make sure to include such an activity in your rehearsal plan.

Don't assume that because you understand the connection between a song and the Scripture passage, the whole choir will understand. You may have to make it clear to them. Our church choir recently sang "Lord, You Have Come to the Lakeshore" (*The United Methodist Hymnal*, 344) for worship. The gospel reading for that Sunday was Luke 5:1-11, in which Jesus helps the soon-to-be disciples with their fishing and then calls them to fish for people. We had worked on the hymn for four weeks before we sang it in worship. No mention was made of the Scripture it was tied to or how it would be used in worship. At least one member said that he didn't understand what some parts of the song meant. If the Scripture connection had been made in the early stages of learning that song, the whole choir would probably have had a better understanding of the song and would have communicated that meaning more effectively to the congregation in worship. This is especially true any time the anthem is new or different and the Scripture or seasonal connection is less than obvious.

• *Incorporate the means of grace into the choir experience.*

We have already discussed how to use many of the means in and through the choir experience. As you plan your weekly rehearsal, see how your choir is already using the means of grace in the rehearsal. Do you pray at the opening or closing of rehearsal? Do you encourage choir members to worship fully and worship together as a small group when appropriate? Do you plan for times of Christian conversation in the rehearsal?

Once you have determined what you are already doing, think about how you might increase your use of the means of grace in the rehearsal. One director that I spoke with suggested that you start with your own spiritual experience. The means of grace are tools to encounter and be in relationship with God. If we approach the spiritual life of the choir as one might approach the dinner hour, armed with a dozen or so spiritual recipes to try, we may be less than successful. Don't experiment with spiritual cookbooks, she suggests. What works in your own spiritual experience is the best place to start.

After reflecting on your own personal experience with the disciplines, try integrating some of these means into your rehearsal plan. A sample plan for a one-and-a-half-hour rehearsal could look like this:

Warm-up	5 minutes	
Opening prayer	1 minute	
"Majesty, Worship His Majesty"	10 minutes	—Sing through the opening pages as a reminder of what we already know. —Work on the middle section, especially when the contrasting song is added. —Remind them that this song is for Transfiguration Sunday, the time when Jesus first revealed his true identity to the disciples.
"Blest Are They"	15 minutes	—Polish for Sunday. —Check last refrain for parts, especially men's part. —Work on soprano/alto verse; have altos lean into their dissonant notes. —Have soloists sing their verses with refrain. —Ask for any problem spots. —Sing through whole song. Check for transition problems.
"How Firm a Foundation"	10 minutes	—Work on men's parts in the second verse. —Add the women's parts. —Sing through to the end. —Remind them of last week's work.
"Blessed Assurance"	5 minutes	—Introduce this piece to the choir; read-through only.
Group building/ Christian conversation	5 minutes	—Turn to your neighbor and tell of a time in your life when you became aware of and were assured by Jesus' love for you.

"Alleluia"	10 minutes	—Work on first two pages. —Work on last page. —Explain that this is an anthem for the opening of Easter Sunday service.
"I Will Arise and Go to Jesus"	10 minutes	—Work on Stanza 2 and refrain, especially the page turn back to the refrain work on Stanza 3, especially the change in meter. —Work the transition between second refrain and third verse. —Sing to the end.
"What Wondrous Love Is This"	4 minutes	—Introduce this piece to the choir; read-through only.
Closing worship	15 minutes	—Prayer concerns. —Read through Scripture for Sunday, Luke 6:20-26. Ask choir to follow along with the text in the anthem. Note difference between the text in "Blest Are They," based on the Matthew version of this text, and the Luke passage. —Invite them to consider silently how they might live in a way that the kingdom Jesus describes shows in their lives. —Group prayer led by a choir member. —Sing through anthem for Sunday.
Announcements	1 minute	—Choir party. —Announce plans for choir to cook dinner and lead in a brief worship at the homeless shelter in two weeks.
Dismissal with blessing		—Send the choir forth with God's blessings to love God and their neighbors in all they do.

Note a few things as you consider this sample rehearsal. First, the means of grace are integrated into the whole of the rehearsal, not segregated into their own segments. As director you don't need to announce, "Okay, now we will have a time of Christian formation." The formation happens in and in response to the music you are learning and the people you are working with.

Second, the means do not have to happen in this setting alone. The choir in the above example is planning a specific act of mercy as a group, not during the rehearsal but at another time. Part of your work is to help the choir members live out their discipleship in their daily lives, not just at church. Acts of mercy apart from the choir experience underscore this truth and provide opportunities for the choir to live out their faith.

Third, look at the amount of time spent on intentional formation as opposed to musical training. The work of learning the music still receives the majority of the time in the rehearsal. The work of Christian formation takes a small but important role in the overall task of the choir rather than taking over the entire rehearsal time.

Finally, notice that the director is responsible for only part of the formation. Certainly selecting the music and making the first connection between music and worship is your task. However, the choir members will take your lead and respond to you and one another, thus participating in their own spiritual formation experience. You will be shaped by the spirituality of your choir members even as you shape their formation. Allow members to live out their spiritual gifts in the choir. Invite them to lead prayer. Encourage them to organize acts of mercy. Provide opportunities for them to talk with each other one-on-one and as a group.

If you have read and discussed this book with a trusted group from your choir, invite them to brainstorm other ways to integrate the means of grace into your choir experience.

- *TRY IT WITH ALL AGES AND TYPES OF CHOIRS.*

Spirituality is appropriate for all choirs, not just the adult choir. Children's choirs are a wonderful place to introduce the spiritual disciplines because children are so open to new experiences and are willing to try almost anything. Disciplines that you teach them now will help them relate to God their whole lives.

I was the children's choir clinician in the Little Rock Annual Conference several years ago. We selected "Song for Beginnings," by Kevin Riehle, as one of the anthems. Aside from being a charming song for children to sing, it also contained many wonderful messages of God's great love for and protection of us.

As I analyze a piece of music to teach to children, I determine what message I want them to hear in the music. Then I think about the creative ways I can present this message to them. For this piece, I decided to let individual choir members read the various Scriptures on which the song is based. As one child read, I asked the children to see if they could find that Scripture in the song. They found it quickly and easily. I repeated the same method with each of the verses, using different readers each time.

Then I asked if there were any words in the song that they didn't know or understand. One of the lines in the song uses the image "watermark of grace." The children were unfamiliar with the word *watermark*, as I suspected they would be. I said to the children, "When you buy really nice paper—not the notebook paper you use at school but the paper your mom or dad uses to write really important notes—look at the paper carefully." I held a piece of paper up to the light. "When you look inside the paper, you can see a picture or a monogram or something that has actually been made inside the paper." I passed around several different examples for them to look at. As they were looking, I continued: "These pictures are called watermarks, and they are made by the person who made the paper. They only put watermarks in really nice paper, paper they want everyone to know was made by them and belongs to their family of paper. When you were made by God, God put a watermark inside of you, too. And if I could hold each of you up against the light, and if I could see through you like I can see through this paper, I would see that watermark. And do you know what it says? 'Created by God with love.' "

In this way, I can teach the song and at the same time reinforce its message (and do something that will keep the children's short attention spans engaged). These children may not remember this song in years to come, but I'll bet they remember what a watermark is and that God loved them enough to create them out of God's great love.

Choirs that do not use song texts can also benefit from spiritual exercises. Patty Gillam at Brooklyn Heights United Methodist Church in Maryland uses hymn devotions with her bell choir ringers. If they are playing a song based on a hymn tune, she uses a meditation based on that hymn text during their rehearsals. If they are playing something original, she chooses a devotion based on a hymn that will be used in worship that Sunday. In this manner, she connects the work of the rehearsal with the worship that the bell choir will be leading and participating in.

As you plan spiritual activities for your choirs, make sure these activities are age-appropriate for the members attending.

- *TRY IT, AND STICK WITH IT.*

The introduction of a spiritual aspect into choir rehearsals will be a new experience for many of your choir members. Depending on their own journeys and spiritual types, they may be overjoyed to experience an integration of their spirituality with their church work. They may have sensed that something was missing for them from the overall choral experience. They may appreciate the challenge to move forward on their spiritual journey, and they will listen openly to the spiritual experience of others. If this is the primary response from your choir members, count yourself fortunate and move forward with your formation plans.

You may also encounter resistance from members for whom intentional spiritual formation is a new experience. These people aren't unchristian; they may just be uncomfortable expressing their personal experiences to others. They may also resist any change in the rehearsal format.

At the end of one rehearsal, I asked the choir members to turn to one another and reflect briefly on how they might live in such a way that the kingdom of heaven would be evident in our world today. One singer responded, "Can't we just sing the anthem and go home?" Her question could have stemmed from the fact that I didn't phrase my question in a way that engaged her. She could have had a long, strenuous day at work and wanted to go home to bed. She also might not have understood or appreciated the value of such discussion.

Listen to people who express such concerns. Discuss the concerns with your close advisers and make sure you are not imposing a format that is not conducive to Christian formation. If choir members with concerns are open to the idea, invite them to tell you some about their own journey. Explore the concerns, but give your ideas a real chance to work before abandoning them as a lost cause. Remember Debi's choir in Virginia, the group that started evening prayers? It took six months before the majority of the choir members understood the power and value of group worship.

Many choir members will want you to stretch them but not push them too far out of their comfort zones. They won't mind praying with the group, and some will even lead the group in prayer. Some would love an opportunity to tell their own story to others in the choir; others will run the other direction at the mere suggestion of telling their stories. Lead them as you can, then entrust them to the creative, moving power of God to work within them.

You may also encounter resistance from other members of your church staff. A choir director I interviewed said that her church was strong in social action. The rest of the staff "weren't much into the interior life," as she put it. It is as if they believe that practicing the spiritual disciplines is a mere substitute for real Christianity, which for them is social action. Some congregations take strong and prophetic stands on justice and social issues, and they are right to do so. However, social action without the partnership of a deep relationship with God is less effective and less important than it might be with the renewing breath of God filling it with life and meaning.

You may also encounter some subtle (or not so subtle) resistance in yourself. The director I described above told me about her own resistance to being a spiritual leader. "When a member died in a car accident, the choir came to me for spiritual leadership," she said. "I felt uncomfortable with this." Yet she is also aware of how she is growing in her role as spiritual leader as well as music enabler. To offset her discomfort, she prays and hopes that her own devotional life and self-awareness can help her fulfill this responsibility and keep her own ego out of God's way.

These means to a deeper relationship with God are time-tested and true. If you trust in them and the power of the Holy Spirit to work within you and your choir, you are choosing to grow in your discipleship.

Incorporating Spirituality in the Choir: A Cost Analysis

I have already alluded to some of the costs of adding a spiritual component to your music ministry. Certainly the first casualty will be time. You will have to restructure your rehearsal in order to incorporate Christian formation into the regular rehearsal plan. This change may take some time away from learning music. In addition, if you have been leading choirs for a while now, rehearsal planning the way you do it now may be second nature to you, requiring little thought. To change that rehearsal practice will require you to think about the rehearsal in a new way, and it may take you a while to adjust to this new way of planning. In addition, you may encounter resistance to any change, much less a change of this kind and this potential personal nature. If you are accustomed to almost sole leadership of the choir, allowing members of the choir to sometimes take the lead may be disconcerting to you. On the other hand, if you feel uncomfortable with your role as spiritual leader, you may have to step outside your personal comfort zone in order to fulfill that role. As you use the means of grace in the choir setting, you may encounter other costs that are unexpected and unforeseeable. All of these costs, including the unexpected ones, should be taken into consideration as you contemplate adding or enhancing a formational aspect in your rehearsals.

But what are the benefits? Directors who have incorporated Christian formation into their rehearsals name several. Many I have talked with say that their choir sings the anthems with a greater sense of understanding and a more worshipful spirit. Rosemary Collins in Clearwater, Florida, says that talking intentionally about the text and encouraging the choir to make the words their own has helped the choir grow in its ability to express the music verbally, musically, and even in their facial expressions as they sing. Her choir at Heritage United Methodist Church now sings with insight, and the congregation really gets what the music is all about. Patty Gillam describes the effect in this manner: "At the end of a powerful anthem there is a spiritual amen; at the end of a praise anthem an audible or spiritual amen." She attributes this fact to the intentional focus on spirituality and nurture in the choir.

The benefits are also apparent in relationships among choir members. The general attitude of choir members toward one another and in what they bring to worship is greatly improved, according to Nancy Kilpin in Burlington, Wisconsin. Another director states, "The more people are aware of God's love in their lives, the more God's love is shared among the choir." Many directors see their choirs growing in care of one another, initiating works of compassion and mercy toward people when they might not have done these things before.

Helping the choir members grow in their own spiritual journeys has allowed some directors to share responsibility for their care and nurture with other caring members, thus freeing the director for other work. The shepherding program described in Chapter 7 is a good example of this shared-leadership approach.

So, is it worth our effort to change and to help our choir members grow to be disciples rather than just members of our churches? "If we don't do it [intentional Christian formation], there are greater costs," asserts James Lyon, director of music at Colonial Heights United Methodist Church in Kingsport, Tennessee.

Integrating the means of grace into your choral experience may not change the surface of your rehearsals. The schedule may shift only slightly; you will still help your choir learn the music as you did before. However, the substance of your choir rehearsals will change dramatically. As you offer people the chance to be in deeper relationship with God and one another, the tone and nature of your work together will gradually shift from good work to ministry in the name of Jesus. I pray that you will be the leader in such a shift.

Questions for Reflection and Discussion

1. In what ways are you already incorporating Christian formation into your choir rehearsals with adults? with children? with youth?

2. What positive effects do you think incorporating intentional Christian formation into your choir rehearsals will have on the life of your choir? What negative effects could it have?

3. What resistance do you anticipate from yourself and others if you become more intentional about the task of making disciples in the choir rehearsal?

4. How do you think your choir would respond to choir activities (such as specific acts of mercy, spiritual formation retreats, and so forth) away from the normal rehearsal and worship schedule? Why, do you think, would they respond in this manner?

5. What steps are you willing to commit to trying today in order to make your choir experience a place where Christian disciples are made, formed, and sent into the world?

CHAPTER 12:

Doing and Being: The Art of Balance

The first time I can remember losing my balance was when I was learning to ride a bike without training wheels. I rode in circles around my driveway. On a tight turn, I toppled over, banging my head on the concrete with a resounding crack. I ran crying to my mother. Upon seeing no blood and no visible swelling, she sent me away with assurances of swift recovery. I had a headache for over an hour (a long time for a five-year-old). I wasn't sure I would ever ride a bike again.

I didn't realize at the time that keeping my balance would be a life-long endeavor. Balance between school work and play. Balance between time with family, time with friends, and time alone. Balance between work and leisure, between activity and rest, between healthy food and junk food. And balance between doing and being.

My own entry into a more spiritual life (as I described in Chapter 2) revealed an internal conflict between doing and being. I had always valued myself for what I did rather than for who I was as a loved child of God. Therefore, it followed that I thought others also valued me solely for what I did. So, when I couldn't do all that I thought I should do, I suffered from a typical overachiever's dilemma: I am not worth anything; or at least, I am worth very little. I had lost balance between doing and being.

A Biblical Story

I am certainly not the first or the last to suffer from such a conflict. In Luke 10:38-42, Jesus is visiting with his dear friends Martha and Mary. He is talking and laughing with them. He is teaching them in that special way that naturally gifted teachers do, when those being taught are enjoying themselves so much that they don't realize they are being taught. Mary sits at the Teacher's feet, caught up in all that he is saying.

Martha, on the other hand, is busy in the kitchen. After all, it is her home that they are gathered in. There are guests to host and food to prepare. She has no time to sit and listen to what Jesus has to say. I can almost hear her thoughts as she rattles pans in the kitchen, *Where is that lazy sister of mine? Doesn't she know there is work to be done?* The rattling gets louder and louder in that passive-aggressive way that begs to be noticed but doesn't want to have to speak the need aloud.

Finally, she can stand no more. "Lord, do you not care that my sister has left me to do all the work by myself? Tell her then to help me" (verse 40). She appears to be saying, "If you want to have dinner sometime this week, you'd better send in someone to help." She also seems resentful of the possibility that she may not be valued for all that she is doing. "Notice what I am doing," she appears to say, "and value me for it."

Jesus surprises her by siding with Mary: "Martha, Martha, you are worried and distracted by many things; there is need of only one thing. Mary has chosen the better part, which will not be taken away from her" (verse 41). For Jesus, the being is more important than the doing in this instance. "Do not let the tasks of being hospitable get in the way of participating in the relationship," Jesus is conveying.

We are not told what happens next in this story. In my imagination, I can see Jesus admonishing Martha gently, with a loving smile. As the words sink in, he extends his hand to her and offers her a place of honor close to him so that she can participate in the conversation and catch up on what she has missed. Far from being devalued for what she is doing, she is honored so greatly that he doesn't want to miss her presence. And then, at the proper time, Jesus slaps his hands on his thighs and exclaims "I'm hungry! Let's all go in and get the meal on the table. If we all work together, it will only take five minutes!"

Jesus is not discounting the value of doing. On the contrary, Jesus highly favors an active, "doing" approach to discipleship. Note the context of this story. Luke places this experience immediately following the parable of the good Samaritan, the epitome of faith in action. For Jesus, the art of discipleship is a good balance between doing and being. Being is important when relationship with God and neighbor is best served by reflection, meditation, and conversation; and doing is appropriate when the Kingdom is best proclaimed by action and hard work. With us, the art of discipleship and being an effective spiritual leader of others also lies in the art of balance.

Balance in Your Personal Life

Self-help books and articles abound with suggestions for achieving balance in our lives. Working moms and dads are encouraged to find time for themselves in exercise classes, aroma therapy, and letting go of unrealistic expectations. We read how to eat a balanced diet, how to balance work and home, how to balance our checkbooks, and how to still have time for ourselves. Balance is a big issue for many of us today.

This is especially true of those of us who are called into ministry. If we are employed full-time in a church, there is always something that needs to be done, and often an emergency that calls us away from the tasks at hand. If we work part-time or volunteer our services in the church, the issue of balance gets even more sticky, with our desire to serve God through our church work often overshadowed by those activities we have to do in order to make a living. A friend and colleague recently confessed that she would be much happier if she could be a full-time volunteer, giving her time and energy to her children's school and her family's church rather than to her paid work. Balancing is an art, and many of us are unskilled in this art.

Balance is a skill that, like other skills, can be learned. I offer several suggestions to increase your ability to achieve and maintain balance.

- *Put "First Things First."*

One of the best books I've encountered that helps one determine priorities and achieve balance is *First Things First,* by Stephen R. Covey, A. Roger Merrill, and Rebecca R. Merrill (Simon & Schuster, 1994). The authors invite readers to name the things that are "first things" for us. Then they articulate a strategy for placing those things first in our lives. I read *First Things First* when invited to write an article relating the book's ideas to the task of the church musician. I came away convinced that the authors were right. Since then I have attempted to follow these guidelines for planning my weekly activities. The book offers not another time management strategy to help us do more things but a strategy to help us do the right things.

- *Be clear about your call from God and do (or be) what God calls you to.*

Many of us struggle between many good things. Like children resisting having to choose between soccer and gymnastics because they meet on the same day, we want to do and have it all. In a balanced life, we can neither do nor have it all. The balanced choice, then, is to do what we are uniquely called to do.

I like to do a lot of creative work. I enjoy sewing and other artistic activities. As a children's choir director, I was often tempted to sew all the costumes and make the set for the children's musical myself, just because I could do it (and it often seemed easier to do it myself than to ask someone else to do it). I would later reach the panic stage, in which I stayed up late hours trying to do everything I had planned before I could learn to ask others for help. I eventually learned that God was not calling me to do everything, only those things that I am uniquely gifted to do. Several people in the church had skills in sewing and set making (many of whom were much more gifted than I), but I was the only one who could effectively select the music and teach it to the children. I needed balance between what I needed to do and what I needed to delegate.

I know of (and am related to) clergy who do it all for their church: preaching, visiting, teaching Bible study, emptying the trash, painting the floors, changing the light bulbs, and the list goes on. Many times, they will complete all of these tasks, look around, and wonder why the members don't notice when a light is left on and turn it off, or, more importantly, notice when someone is in the hospital and visit that person. These clergy have done it all for the church, so much so that the church has come to depend on them doing it all. While I would be the first to be suspicious of a pastor who even thought about being too good to attend to ordinary tasks, I would also wonder about this person's sense of partnership in ministry as well as his or her ability to share leadership with others in the church. In order to be more balanced in our ministry, we are called to live out our giftedness and to share leadership so that others can live out their giftedness. This requires understanding what God has uniquely called us to do.

This giftedness criteria doesn't release anyone from the call to be in ministry in the world as a baptized Christian. Music ministry does not totally fulfill this call. But a leader in music ministry needs to do first those things that only he or she can do for the ministry, then ask others to act out their giftedness in partnership with the leader.

- *REMEMBER THAT YOU DO NOT DO ANYTHING ALONE OR UNDER YOUR OWN POWER.*

One of the most common mistakes church leaders make is acting as if we do everything under our own power. We steam ahead, doing all that we can, overextending ourselves as if by our own strength we can bring about God's kingdom today. We may not speak those beliefs aloud, but our actions speak infinitely louder than our words.

Consider those whom God calls to important tasks in the Bible. A man and woman, childless and long past their parenting years, become the parents of God's people. A man who speaks poorly stands before Pharaoh and demands release for God's children. A boy armed with nothing but a slingshot and rock takes on a well-trained warrior giant. A young girl engaged to a Narazene carpenter. A bunch of rough fishermen. A zealot against Christianity. All of these people, on the surface, were the last ones eligible for the jobs God had in mind; yet God chose them intentionally so that God's power and grace could be communicated to the world through their weaknesses.

We are able to minister to others not because of our own strength and power but because God has gifted us with skills and abilities to be in ministry on God's behalf. If we rely on that power instead of our own, we can trust in the presence of the Holy Spirit to guide, empower, and sustain us.

Balance With the Choir

The purpose of music ministry in the church is multifaceted, to be sure. Making music and preparing music for worship is a huge part of the choir's task. If it were not for that work, the choir would be a Sunday school class or other small-group experience. The choir's task is also to provide an arena in which Christian formation and service can take place. If it were not for this focus, the church choir might as well be a civic chorus. The nature of church music requires that the spiritual leader hold these two aspects of the choir's task in tension with each other, not favoring one over the other but allowing each its rightful place in the choral program.

Maintaining balance between these two parts of the choir's task may require letting go of some expectations. The church choir is primarily a volunteer organization, with members ranging in musical skill from the professional singer to the willing but vocally challenged participant. In order to provide time and space for Christian formation, you as spiritual leader may have to give up some music rehearsal time for Christian conversation, worship, or another formational activity. For those of us who have been taught that God deserves our best musical efforts in worship, letting go may be difficult. However, if we remember that God is calling us to be in relationship—with God and with one another—then the expectation for musical excellence can appropriately take second place when necessary to allow time for Christian formation.

And Finally, My Sisters and Brothers

These means of grace are not God, to be worshiped in and of themselves; they are instead ways of being in relationship with God. Based on the real experiences of Christians throughout the centuries who have sought a closer relationship with God, they give us a reliable map to follow so that we too might be in relationship with God. They start where we are and take us into closer, deeper, eternal relationship with God. They provide the necessary compass heading that keeps us on the right path even when our own senses are confused by overwhelming schedules, the many demands of our complicated lives, and the easy lure of the world to rely on our own power rather than the power of the One who is all-powerful.

The invitation is clear. God who created us and gifted us for ministry is calling us into deeper relationship with God. The tools we need for the journey are available and at hand. We have trusted companions to walk with us, people whom we can lead and be led by, people we are honored to serve and work beside. And we can begin and continue this journey with this assurance: that the God who calls us and sends us into ministry in the church and in the world will provide exactly what we need in order to fulfill that call, for God does not call us anywhere where God's grace will not be present to sustain us. Thanks be to God! Happy traveling.

Questions for Reflection and Discussion

1. Describe a time when you felt that you had lost your balance.

2. In the story about Mary, Martha, and Jesus, which character can you better identify with? Why?

3. Do you often feel the tension between doing and being in your life? In what areas of your life do you most keenly feel such tension?

4. What are your "first things"? Is your relationship with God a "first thing"? Are you willing to reassess those things and the amount of time you allow for them in order to put them first?

5. What ministries or activities do you feel that God is both calling and gifting you to do? In what areas of your current ministries and activities are you unsure of God's call to you?

6. In what ways do you try to do it all under your own power rather than trusting in God's grace to empower and sustain you?

7. What are you willing to commit to today that will help you achieve better balance in your life—spiritually, socially, mentally, and emotionally?

Resources for the Journey:
Suggested Reading for Personal and Corporate Spiritual Growth

Personal Spiritual Growth: Books

Alone With God: A Guide for Personal Retreats, a Workbook, by Ron DelBene, Mary Montgomery, Herb Montgomery (Upper Room Books, 1997).

Calming the Restless Spirit: A Journey Toward God, by Ben Campbell Johnson (Upper Room Books, 1997).

Celebration of Discipline: The Path to Spiritual Growth, by Richard J. Foster (HarperCollins Publishers, revised 1988).

Concerning the Inner Life, by Evelyn Underhill (Oneworld Publications, 1995).

Dimensions of Prayer: Cultivating a Relationship With God, by Douglas Van Steere (Upper Room Books, 1997).

Further Along the Road Less Traveled: The Unending Journey Toward Spiritual Growth, by M. Scott Peck (Simon and Schuster, Inc., 1993; 2nd edition Touchstone Books, 1998).

Invitation to a Journey: A Road Map for Spiritual Formation, by M. Robert Mulholland, Jr. (Intervarsity Press, 1993).

Journaling: A Spirit Journey, by Anne Broyles (Upper Room Books, 1988).

Journeying Through the Days: A Calendar and Journal for Personal Reflection (Upper Room Books, yearly).

Making All Things New: An Invitation to the Spiritual Life, by Henri J. M. Nouwen (Walker & Company, 1986).

Meditation in Motion, by Susan Annette Muto (Doubleday & Company, Inc., 1986).

Prayer: Finding the Heart's True Home, by Richard J. Foster (Harper San Francisco, 1992).

Shaped by the Word: The Power of Scripture in Spiritual Formation, by M. Robert Mulholland, Jr. (Upper Room Books, 1985).

Soul Feast: An Invitation to the Christian Spiritual Life, by Marjorie J. Thompson (Westminster John Knox Press, 1995).

The Life God Blesses, by Gordon MacDonald (Thomas Nelson, Inc., 1994).

The Road Less Traveled, by M. Scott Peck (Simon & Schuster, 1998).

The Road Less Traveled and Beyond: Spiritual Growth in an Age of Anxiety, by M. Scott Peck (Simon and Schuster, Inc., 1997).

The Spiritual Life: Great Spiritual Truths for Everyday Life, by Evelyn Underhill (Oneworld Publications, 1994).

When the Heart Waits, by Sue Monk Kidd (Harper San Francisco, 1991).

Personal Spiritual Growth: Periodicals

Alive Now! (Upper Room).

Weavings (Upper Room).

Daily Devotional Guides

A Guide to Prayer for Ministers and Other Servants, by Rueben Job and Norman Shawchuck (Upper Room Books, 1983).

A Guide to Prayer for All God's People, by Rueben Job and Norman Shawchuck (Upper Room Books, 1990).

The Upper Room Disciplines (Upper Room Books, yearly).

Books on Group Spirituality

Covenant Discipleship: Christian Formation Through Mutual Accountability, by David Lowes Watson (Discipleship Resources, 1991).

Discover Your Spiritual Type: A Guide to Individual and Congregational Growth, by Corinne Ware (Alban Institute, 1995).

Transforming Church Boards Into Communities of Spiritual Leaders, by Charles M. Olsen (Alban Institute, 1995).

Devotional Books for Choirs

Amazing Grace: 366 Inspiring Hymn Stories for Daily Devotions, by Kenneth W. Osbeck (Kregel Publications, 1990).

The One Year Book of Hymns: 365 Devotional Readings Based on Great Hymns of the Faith, Robert K. Brown and Mark R. Norton, editors (Tyndale House Publishers, Inc., 1995).

With Every Note I Sing: Prayers for Music Ministers and Those Who Love to Sing, by David Haas (G.I.A. Publications).

Miscellaneous

CROSS-PATHS Ministries, Roger C. Dowdy, Worship and Music Consultant, 3410 Plymouth Place, Lynchburg, VA 24503-1301. Retreat and worship leader.